A Tour in Dalmatia, Albania, and Montenegro

With an Historical Sketch of the Republic of Ragusa, From the Earliest Times Down to Its Final Fall

A Tour in Dalmatia, Albania, and Montenegro

With an Historical Sketch of the Republic of Ragusa, From the Earliest Times Down to Its Final Fall

WILLIAM WINGFIELD

COSIMOCLASSICS

NEW YORK

A Tour in Dalmatia, Albania, and Montenegro
Cover © 2007 Cosimo, Inc.

For information, address:

Cosimo, P.O. Box 416
Old Chelsea Station
New York, NY 10113-0416

or visit our website at:
www.cosimobooks.com

A Tour in Dalmatia, Albania, and Montenegro
was originally published in 1859.

Cover design by www.kerndesign.net

ISBN: 197-8-160206-288-7

PREFACE.

THE following Letters were written abroad in the seclusion of a retired, though archiepiscopal town in Southern Austria, where the author had been several years resident, without access to English authors, except some very few volumes, which he happened to have brought with him.

His first idea was to detail certain facts at the crisis of 1853-4, relative to the condition of Christians in a Turkish province. Secondly, to draw attention to the *Slave* nationalities,* important

* On the eastern shores of the Adriatic.

from their connexion with that widely-
extended family of which Russia is the
acknowledged head. And thirdly, to
describe an interesting Tour which any
one might make, who, in these travelling days, found himself with a month
or six weeks to spare, at Trieste or
Fiume.

The historical sketch of Ragusa was
undertaken to illustrate one of the
Letters, and give some slight account
—not hitherto, so far as the author
knows, attempted in English—of the
earliest cultivation of the Slave language,
by the Italianized inhabitants of that
Republic. To this subject the author,
having devoted some time and study,
proposes on a future occasion to revert,
should he meet with sufficient encou-
ragement.

CONTENTS.

EIGHT LETTERS.

I.

V.

VI.

VII.

VIII.

HISTORICAL SKETCH OF RAGUSA.

A TOUR IN DALMATIA, ALBANIA,

AND MONTENEGRO.

A TOUR IN DALMATIA,

&c.

--- -- ======

I.

It was in the autumn of 1853, that, intending to make the tour of Dalmatia and Montenegro, I descended from Agram, over the
mountains which separate Croatia from the
sea, to Fiume on the Adriatic,—a cheerful
little maritime emporium, containing about
16,000 souls, and in a word a sort of Trieste
Secunda (Trieste Prima, however, being just
four times as large). It was heretofore the
seaport of the Magyar nation, to whom it

belonged, while the kingdom of Hungary continued in its former integrity. But since the revolution of 1848-9, this has ceased. Croatia, when the European convulsions were over, obtained the dignity of a separate province of the Austrian empire, and thus Fiume became once more a Croatian, instead of Hungarian dependency. As the steamer did not leave until the Monday following (it was then Saturday), there was plenty of time to see whatever there might be of interest in Fiume, and to ascend to the famous convent of Tersatto—so called from the Roman Tersatica—which occupies the heights almost immediately above.

There is not, however, much to detain a traveller in Fiume. Some vestiges of old Roman buildings said to exist I failed to find, but with a paper-mill belonging to Mr. Smith (an Englishman, it is almost needless to add) I was more fortunate. It lies in a highly romantic situation at the foot of the precipice over which frown the ruins of the castle of

Tersatto, now the property of Count Nugent, formerly the stronghold of the celebrated Frangepani, lords of the surrounding country and founders of the adjacent convent. The works of the mill are turned by a river, the origin of the name of the town—in Illyrian Rèka—which flows, like most of the streams in this line of country, ready made out of the hollow mountains some distance off, and comes down through a wild, savage gully, until within a few hundred yards of the factory, where a depth of water sufficient for the purpose is drawn off into a long tunnel, large enough to walk in, cut through the solid rock. Further description is unnecessary. Such mills are no rarities *out* of Austria, and I probably should have missed seeing this had it not been so strikingly placed at the foot of the Tersatto heights, and for the good word of the Austrian commandant, who declared nobody had seen anything in Fiume unless he had been over " Herrn Schmidt's Fabrik ! " At night I found my way to the theatre, where " Maria Stuarda, translated into Italian from the German of Schiller by Cav^{re.} Maffei," was announced for performance. For the moderate entrance fee of 4*d.* in *paper* money, I was admitted into a handsome Italian theatre, scarcely less than that at Trieste, heard some pretty music, and saw some fair acting, especially on the part of a clever young prima donna—a Marie of course —who, notwithstanding a little over-acting, contrived to draw thunders of applause from her audience in the scene with Elizabeth, at the words of the climax, " I Britanni sono ingannati d'una Bastarda." Davidson and the gist of Schiller's character of Elizabeth was of course omitted, the curtain falling on Leicester's *remorse* as he hears the drums announcing Mary's beheadal !

But the objects of interest to be seen at Fiume lie upon its cliffs. There is the spot whereon the sacred house of Loretto is said to have paused on its journey from Nazareth to Italy ; there the old Frangepan castle, the prison of the Turks in the sixteenth and seventeenth centuries; and thence the lovely view across the Quarnero and Istria. Accordingly early in the day I faced the steep ascent. Crossing the long wooden bridge over the " Fiumara,"—a generic name for rivers in these parts,—which skirts the town on the south, and then turning to the left along the commencement of the magnificent road to Carlstadt, called after the Archduchess Maria Louisa, a stone gateway marks where interminable flights of steps lead up to the heights above. At the top is a little plain, occupied by a white church with Franciscan convent attached. The former, a neat unpretending edifice, pointing out the spot where the holy house was set down by the angels and stood during the three and a half years that it remained; the latter in the same style and in fact coeval with the church; both offerings of the Frangepani from the neighbouring castle, built almost contemporaneously to commemorate the far-famed event.

The history of this celebrated miracle, according to the received account, is as follows:—The house of the Blessed Virgin at Nazareth, and more especially *the chamber* in which the Annunciation took place, was held in veneration amongst believers from the earliest periods of the Christian era; so that in the fourth century, when the Roman empire professed Christianity, the Empress Helena, mother to Constantine the Great, built a church over it for its preservation. Thus it remained, frequented by pilgrims and worshippers, until the latter end of the thirteenth century, and the impending desecration of the Holy Land by the Turks, who in the April of 1291 destroyed Tripoli, and ravaged as far as Acre; when on the 10th of May of that same year, one calm, fine midnight, on the Saturday of the Ascension, the sacred house or chamber suddenly appeared in the little plain, " Raunizza " in the Slave language, " by the side of a small valley," "Dolatz," in the garden of a widow by name

"Agatha." At the same time a vision announced its arrival to the "Parroco," or curè, who, being in a weak state of health, was healed together with many others during the brief period of its sojourn. But "on the 12th of December, 1294, in the midst of a stormy night," it was again borne away and finally deposited at Loretto on the opposite coast of Italy. Nicholas Frangepani, the contemporary castellan and Ban of Croatia, resolving to test the truth of the story, with this object despatched certain trustworthy messengers, including the parish priest, who had been cured, and two or three other persons of distinction, to Nazareth, to ascertain whether the sacred house, so long the object of Christian veneration in those parts, had been removed as reported. They performed their mission and returned, corroborating the already prevalent belief. They had found, they said, the church built by St. Helena, but the holy house was no longer within it; nay, an arch of the former was broken to admit of its

B

removal. Accordingly the Ban protocolled the history in all the neighbouring towns of his dominions, caused a short notice of it to be inscribed on a stone still existing in a chapel on the ascent, and at his death, which occurred shortly afterwards, left a sum of money to found the church and convent.* In the cloisters I was joined by the Superior, with whom I had some previous acquaintance, and who came now to offer his services to conduct me to see the ruins of the castle and the view from a little terrace on the edge of the cliff, beneath which expand the waters of the Quarnero, the ancient Sinus Flanaticus, almost landlocked by the coasts of Istria and Dalmatia, and the islands of Veglia and Cherso. The azure flood sparkled in the rays of the morning sun. To our left we could watch its myriads of bright ripples, until they were lost round the rock of St. Mark, and the wide-spread dazzling mirror

* See "Triumphus Coronatæ Reginæ Tersactensis, à C. Pasconi." Venice, 1731.

darkened as it narrowed into the canal of
Maltempo. To our right stretched the rocky
margin of Istria until it disappeared in the
horizon, where the sky and the sea blended
their harmonising colours together, while
Monte Maggiore and the advanced guard of
the Julian Alps closed in the well-wooded
landscape of the shore. Along the foreground, above Fiume, an old time-worn wall
still stood, which had once served, according
to local tradition, to mark the boundary
between the empires of Honorius and Arcadius. I was told that there were other
vestiges in the neighbouring churches of
times not less remote.

Thence we walked to the old castle, once
a formidable stronghold, and the prison of
Turks, now a ruin, hanging amongst stupendous
precipices over the Fiumara. All that remains
belongs to Count Nugent, one of the Irish
family of that name, and a marshal in the
Austrian service. He has converted, with
questionable (or *not* questionable?) taste, the

B 2

centre into a Greek mausoleum, and the dun-
geons, still retaining their rings and chains,
into a burial vault for his family ! The race
of its ancient lords for so many centuries is
extinct. They were one of the many old
families residing on this coast since Roman
times, and not of the least illustrious stock.
Their origin they traced to the patrician
" gens Anicia," or the unconquered, an appellation well suited to the haughty kings, consuls, and Cæsars, which ennobled it in the
annals of the proud republic. It earned a better
reputation in after—that is in Christian—
times, by the saints, popes, bishops, and men
eminent for their piety and learning, who
sprang from it. Thus, for example :—

"Probus Anicius" was that prefect, who,
dismissing St. Ambrose to his *civil* post at
Milan, said, prophetically, as proved by
the event, "Go, not as a judge, but as
bishop." He was consul with the Emperor
Gratian, A.D. 371. St. Jerome, in his letter
to the nun Demetria, calls her of the Anician

family; and St. Augustine does the same by Proba and Juliana. To them also belonged St. Felix, second pope of that name, in the fourth century; and St. Gregory the Great, in the sixth. Of them were SS. George, Paulinus, Benedict, and Scholastica. From the same stock branched the Ursini at Rome, the Michaeli at Venice, and lastly, the house of Rudolph of Hapsburgh in Austria.

It was not until the eighth century that one of them obtained the charitably sounding name, "a Frangepanibus." In the year of our Lord 717, the Tiber having overflowed its banks at Rome, many of the citizens were rescued from the flood in the boats of "Flavius Anicius," who added to his work of beneficence by distributing bread amongst the sufferers. His surname, "Frangepani," sprang from the gratitude of the people. Long afterwards, in the thirteenth century, three brothers of this branch of the family were settled in the island of Veglia, of which they were chief citizens, when Bela IV., King of Hungary, took refuge there from a great Tartar invasion. The Frangepani received him hospitably, and assisted him both with money and an army, by means of which, having defeated the Tartars at Grobnich, he recovered his throne. In reward for these services, he bestowed on them large grants of land on this coast, where the family flourished until its final extinction by the execution of the last of the name for conspiring with Count Zriny to deliver the crown of Hungary to the Sultan, A. D. 1670.

Dining with the monks at Tersatto, I met Padre Buonaventura, a Roman Franciscan, of much information, returning from a twelve years' residence in Albania. The Albanians are Catholics, as they have been from times remote, but very barbarous. Under their Castriott princes, three or four centuries ago, they long maintained an unequal struggle against the Ottoman Porte, but ever since have been subject to that degrading government. Some have become Mussulmans, others pretend to be, in order to escape tribute; but the bulk of the nation is nominally Christian, and not Greek, but Catholic. They retain a language which is quite isolated in their present neighbourhood. Professor Schafarik suggests that they may be the remains of the Thracians described by Herodotus, and therefore a relict of the more ancient inhabitants of Europe. It is curious that they still call their capital (Skutari in Italian) *Scodra*, by which name it first appears in Roman history. Cardinal Mezzofanti could find in his extensive research no cognate language, and thought the only chance of throwing light on the subject would be by the study of the languages of the ancient Pelasgic tribes.

Monday morning, came off at six A.M. in the Barone Kübeck steam-packet. It was a lovely morning, but about eight A.M. a squall of wind overtook us from the north-east, which they call a Neverino. At a distance it made the sea look black, but when we were in the midst of it, the numerous little crested waves

had a white, snow-like appearance. It derives
its name, however, from the snow-clad tops of
the mountains amongst which it is bred, and
are its *cause;* or from its *effect,* which, in
winter and spring, when they are most prevalent, is nearly always a fall of snow on land.
At sea they are dangerous; for the cold air,
pouring like a stream down the narrow gullies
of the Alps upon the Quarnero, capsizes or
drives on the rocky shores the boats which it
encounters before they have time to recover
from the sudden onset. Fatal accidents occur
when they are little anticipated. For instance, quite recently the prevôt of the church
at Segna, expecting his mother and sister
from a neighbouring port, had come down to
the beach, and was watching their boat, as
with a fair wind and bright sky it approached
the shore. In less than half an hour they
would be with him. But that was not to be.
In a moment down came the deadly squall,
the boat was capsized, and every soul on board
perished under the very eyes of their unfor-

tunate relatives, who could render no assistance, although the sea returned presently to
its pristine calm. In fact, half the escapes
which the tablets in the little above-named
church piously attribute to the intercession of
"our Lady of Tersatt," consist in deliverances
from such dangers. No misfortune has
hitherto befallen the Austrian Lloyd's boats,
yet our captain said frankly it was the first
time he had made the voyage so late in the
year, and he hoped it would be the last. The
Adriatic had a bad name of old—"a sea tempestuous and unfaithful," says Sandys;—but
the dominant wind, the "Arbiter Adriæ," is
the scirocco, and comes from the opposite
quarter to these north-easterly gusts.

We now lay under "Zengg" or "Segna,"
a town of that military frontier by means of
which Austria at length, in the seventeenth
century, effectually secured her provinces
against Turkish raids, and whence she has
even now, with little expense or trouble, a
standing army of from sixty to eighty thou-

sand men. Its origin was in the sixteenth
century, when a tax was laid upon the more
distant Austrian provinces as a compensation
to the Croats for the interruption of agricul-
ture which they suffered from the continual
inroads of their Mahometan neighbours. It
consists of a belt of land stretching throughout her Slave provinces, along the whole
Turkish border, within which every man, who
is not a priest, is a soldier, and obliged to do
military service for his land. Each family has
its "stareshina," "haus vater," or "bester
man" (for each appellation in Slave and
German is by turns applied to him), who is
chosen from the members by their own votes.
He appoints to every one his work while they
are not on duty, and is held responsible for all
when the call to arms comes. As thus, several
married couples may be united together under
one "haus vater," and even *one* roof, it falls
by rule to the last arrived amongst the wives
to undertake the main share in the burthens
of domestic economy. This custom, and the

coincidence of the Slave word "stareshina,"
meaning also " eldest," but in the sense of
alderman or senator, without any necessary
reference to age, has given rise to the idea
that in these patriarchal households the domestic government is shared between "the
eldest man and the youngest woman."

Segna was at one time the refuge of the
fierce Uskoks. The origin of this race,
though involved in some obscurity, appears to
have had some resemblance to that of the
Montenegrines. Like them, of Sclavonic race,
and of the disunited Greek Church, they
shared in the same deep and unconquerable
hatred of their Mussulman oppressors, with
whom they vowed perpetual war. From
this circumstance was derived their name,
" Uskok," signifying " transfuga," or " fugitive;" and "v skok" in another dialect in
the same tongue, " galloping." Either
meaning is sufficiently applicable, for they
were fugitives from the Turks, and made
forays into their territory on horseback, escap-

ing by their speed. After the Ottoman conquest, they first held Klissa, a fortress in the mountains of Dalmatia, not far from Salonæ, receiving countenance from the Emperor Ferdinand, the King of Hungary, and Pope Paul V., who all regarded them as one of the outposts of Christendom for resisting the infidels. In 1540, however, the Turks laid siege to Klissa, and having taken it after a long and brave defence of a year's duration, the Uskoks took refuge at Segna, which was given up to them by Ferdinand, having been hitherto a part of the possessions of the Frangepani. Here, further removed from their natural enemies, the Turks, and accustomed by long habits to subsist on piracy, they infested the neighbouring seas, committing depredations on the ships of all nations which navigated the Adriatic, but especially on those of the Venetians; for the latter claimed a maritime supremacy in the Gulf, and considered themselves obliged by their treaty with Constantinople to put down piracy, by which means they incurred the special hatred of these marauders. An internecine war was the result, which is said to have been fomented by the house of Hapsburgh, between whom and the republic there were constant grounds of quarrel. The Uskoks plundered the Venetian merchant-vessels without mercy, and too often slaughtered the crew. On one occasion they murdered a senator, with all his suite, in cold blood. The Venetians and Ragusans hanged the Uskoks whenever they could catch them. At length a fierce war, mainly on this pretext, broke out between Venice and the Archduke Ferdinand, and lasted several years with various success, until the archduke, yielding to the united remonstrances of Southern Europe, pledged himself to put an end by vigorous measures to the piracies of the "refugees." He kept his word, and within a few years * after the conclusion of peace, transported them from the neighbourhood of

* Namely, about A.D. 1620.

the sea, and distributed them over the inland provinces. Three hundred families were
planted amongst the wild hills to the south of
Carniola, in the neighbourhood of Mödling,
where they remain a separate race to this
day, and form a sort of second military frontier, with the same domestic arrangements,
unmixed, but not unchanged. After disturb-
ing the surrounding country during many
years, by their predatory habits and turbu-
lent manners—so graphically described by
Valvasor,, the Carniolan historian of the
seventeenth century—they were at length,
under Maria Theresa, brought into ecclesiastical union with Rome, and have since been
as quiet and orderly as any part of his
imperial majesty's subjects. The only traits
of their origin observable, when I travelled
amongst them a few years ago, were the use
of the Slave liturgy and Greek calendar, the
striking, picturesque costume of the women,
and their handsome Grecian features, remote
alike from Croat and German. Segna is now

a small town, with stone houses, and a castle on the cliff above it.

The merchant from Fiume, and others, here took their leave, and went ashore, while we continued our way. As the day advanced, a heavy scirocco began to blow, which, however, happily did not much affect the sea, on account of the constant island breakwaters; but it made everything look black and sombre. Towards evening we got under shelter of Arbe, the chief place of the island so-called, which retains its mediæval fortifications, though falling into ruins. There is an interesting-looking campanile to the Duomo, in Byzantine style, and about nine churches, besides several convents, mostly ornamented with bell-towers. This marks the decadence of the population, which even in comparatively recent times was eleven, instead of as now, three thousand. It was depopulated by the plague; but, indeed, without this, all the towns hereabouts show evident symptoms of decay, the natural fruits of the failure of the great stream of commerce which used to flow up the Gulf from the East. The Abate Fortis, who made this tour * in the latter days of the republic, remarks on the dispro- portion existing then between the ecclesias- tical establishment, and the population. "For 3,000 very poor inhabitants," he says, "there are no less than six convents, three for either sex, and sixty priests, very slenderly provided." It was at that time also the seat of a bishopric, since removed to Veglia. Hence all these " campanili!" Arbe is, however, reputed a *very* ancient town, not only older than Venice, but renowned, if its inhabitants might be believed, when Rome was yet unheard of; the memory of which they preserve in the doggrel, " Arbe caput mundi, Roma secundi:" but the Venetian Abbé mentions nothing older about it than some inscriptions, which prove it to have been inhabited by cultivated people in classical times. It appears to have passed from the

* Published at Venice, in 2 vols. 4to. 1774.

supremacy of the Eastern empire, together with other cities reckoned to belong to Dalmatia, under that of Venice, and was one of the earliest places in Europe where the silkworm was cultivated, for which purpose they planted the black mulberry, instead of, as now-a-days, the white. Fortis cites a document of A. D. 1018, showing that even so early it was bound to pay a tribute of silk, " seta serica, " or a certain weight of gold to Venice. " The climate," he adds, " is dangerous, owing to its exposure to the blasts of the Bora, which change summer into winter, once destroyed 12,000 beasts left out in the fields in a night, and burnt up the crops like a conflagration; otherwise, the soil is excellent, and they have for exportation fish, grain, oil, wine, silk, cattle, a good breed of horses," &c.

I much wished to have gone ashore; but that was not to be thought of, the sea running high and the wind freshening as night drew on. There was on board an intelligent

c

young man, an Austrian employé from the island, to whom I was indebted for some minor bits of information about it. He was bringing a young wife, a native of Fiume, and his child, four months old, to their future home for the first time—that is, *if* they could get there; for no boat from shore ventured to approach us, so that the disembarkation of my Arban acquaintance and his little family seemed highly problematical, until, seizing the opportunity of a momentary lull, our captain, a kind-hearted man, sent them in his own boat.

While we are passing the night under Arbe, it will not perhaps be without interest to say a little about the language and culture of this and kindred towns on the islands and coast of Dalmatia.

The language of this island, like the rest, is Slave, or more precisely that dialect which is known as Illyrian; but in the town Italian is spoken: and I may notice that this is the characteristic of the whole coast on this side the Gulf; and that not only in the towns which, as Arbe, were long under Venetian rule, but those also which never were thus connected with that republic; such as Fiume, about which one traces a number of characteristics similar to what one finds in the city of the doges itself. Thus the wife of the young man, just gone ashore, was an example in point, having the head-dress, black veil, slippers, manners, and much of the character of a Venetian. And this prevalence of the Italian language and ethos exists, it is to be observed, not only in the maritime cities, but in some which, as Gorizia at the head of the Gulf and the inland towns of Istria, are placed remote from the shore. Slaves occupy the country, the villages, and hamlets; the towns remain, as they always have been, Italian. This is especially conspicuous in the case of Gorizia, which since it came into existence, about the eleventh century, has had no connexion or, heretofore, political sympathy with its Italian neighbours; being always, even during the times of its independence as a separate state, under the influence of the rulers of the house of Austria, with whose dominions it was incorporated about the year 1500. The language of Government is therefore German, which is also taught in the schools; that of the villages around, even within a mile of the town, Slave; the market is, of course, Slave also; nay, the very names of those parts of the town which have been more recently built upon, as of the town itself, are all of Slave origin, while there is a constant immigration amongst the poorer classes from the same element; yet the style of the place, the houses, the costume, the manners of all above the lowest class, are Italian; and Italian, of a dialect reminding one even more than the Tuscan of its Latin original, *i.e.* Forlan, is the language; so decidedly so, that families, who spoke nothing but Slave before they immigrated into the town, lose their original tongue in a generation, and become Italian in spite

of their rulers and their own natural predilections, as far as they have any. Now it is remarkable that this appears from Herodotus to
have been an ancient characteristic of the Slave
nations, viz. to inhabit the country, while more
enterprising foreigners possessed the cities,
especially those of the coast, and carried on
their commercial speculations amongst them;
for he tells us, that in his time the Geloni—
a people of mixed, Scythian and Greek,
origin, but whose culture, indicated by their
temples and rites, was derived from Greece—
inhabited a city on the north of the sea of
Azov, amongst the *Budini,* who were beyond
doubt Slaves, both from their geographical
position and from their nomenclature; for the
name " Budin" is common to this day
amongst the Wend families.

As we descend now more towards the south
of the Gulf, it is well known that, whatever
races may have originally inhabited the circum-
jacent countries, and whatever in consequence
may have been the remote origin of the towns

on the coast, they became sooner or later
Romanised. Some from the beginning were
Roman colonies, some arose, phœnix-like, out
of the ashes of older towns, as Venice and
Grado from Aquileja, and Ragusa from Epidaurus and Salonæ. For everywhere in the
latter days of the empire the Italian inhabitants, flying from their old towns and the
more inland parts before their barbarian invaders, began to take refuge in those spots,
which, by reason of natural or artificial
strength, offered safety to person and property, and whose ready access to the sea
kept open communication with Ravenna and
Constantinople, and preserved to them, even
in those early times, the means of procuring
some of the refinements of more civilized life,
or at least those succours, which devastated
fields and savage neighbours refused. Thus
latterly the once widely extended Roman
" province of Dalmatia " came to consist of
seven such towns on the coast, or in the
islands, viz.—Ragusa, Spalato, Trau, Zara on

the former; and Veglia, Ossero, Arbe in the latter. They retained—as it were, in proof of their descent—(1.) their *language*, though somewhat metamorphosed, the Latin of the classics gradually degenerating, until it caught a new life and again flourished as Italian of the middle ages; (2.) their *superiority* in civilization, by means of which they were enabled to maintain themselves in very difficult circumstances and amongst semi-barbarous neighbours; (3.) their original *political constitutions*, which, springing from the Roman commonwealth, were formed on the republican model, like the other Italian commonwealths of the middle ages.

Hence, as might be expected from their origin and past history, these towns abound in old Italian and Roman families, now often reduced to great poverty. I have already mentioned the Frangepani, as coming from Veglia. Here at Arbe, in 1566, was born, of a family which had already given a pope— Gregory X.—and other illustrious prelates to

Christendom, Mark Anthony de Dominis, himself as renowned as any in the annals of science.

Educated by the Jesuits at Loretto, he was for twenty years one of the order; and during that period professed with great success eloquence, philosophy, and mathematics, in the university at Padua. It was while here that he wrote his celebrated work, " De radiis visûs et lucis in vitreis perspectivis et Iride tractatus," in which the prismatic colours were explained for the first time. The French called him the precursor of Descartes; but our own greater Newton prefers him to the French philosopher, and acknowledges that he himself owed to him his first ideas on the theory of light.

The rest of the history of De Dominis is strange, and it would have been well for his reputation if it had stopped here. But, like some other great natural philosophers, after astonishing the world with his discoveries in science, he surprised it by his escapades

in politics and theology. Having demanded
his secularisation, and left the Society of
Jesus, he was shortly after recommended, by
the Emperor Rudolph, to the vacant bishopric
of Segna, whence he was translated, by the
influence of Venice, to the archbishopric of
Spalato. In the dispute between Venice
and Paul V. he sided with the former, and
wrote a book impugning the doctrines of the
Catholic Church. Next, on the reconciliation
of Venice with Rome, he made overtures to
James I., who received him into England,
appointed him Dean of Windsor and Master
of the Savoy, with precedence next to the
Archbishop of York, besides a pension of
£200 per annum. After enjoying this in-
come for some years, he offended King James
by broaching opinions contrary to the doctrines of the Church of England; and a new
Pope, his own relative, Gregory XV., being
elected, he set himself to work to make up
with him, recanted all he had said or written
unorthodoxly, and begged permission to

return. In the meanwhile he resigned his preferment in England, and made preparations for flight, with all he had amassed during his sojourn. The King, who had private information of his secret intentions, permitted him to set out, but presently arrested his luggage and exposed the wealth he was carrying away with him, which he did not, however, further withhold. De Dominis obtained his pardon, and lived at Rome, neglected and in obscurity. At his death, which occurred shortly afterwards, he professed himself a Catholic, but left papers which were not in accordance with this profession. The character, which he had acquired since he left Padua and gave up the pursuit of science, is best illustrated by the following incident, related to have occurred after his return to Rome. Sir E. Sackvile, afterwards Earl of Dorset, had gone to visit him. He found him shut up in a ground chamber, narrow and dark, and looking out upon a blank wall, about three paces distant. In the course of conversation Sir Edward said to him, " My Lord of Spalato, you have here a dark lodging: it was not so with you in England—there you had, at Windsor, as good a prospect by land as was in all the country; and, at the Savoy, you had the best prospect upon the water that was in all the city." " I have forgot those things," he replied; " here I can best contemplate the kingdom of heaven." Sir Edward was accompanied by Dr. Fitzherbert, rector of the English College, and, moved by this reply, he took his companion aside, and asked him whether he thought the archbishop really was so occupied. Says the Father rector, " I think nothing less; for he was a malecontent knave when he fled from us, a railing knave while he lived with you, and a motley particoloured knave now he is come back." Such was the unsatisfactory end of the Arban De Dominis.*

* See Court of James I., London, 1839. British Critic, January, 1840.

At seven the next morning we were again under weigh, threading our path through the narrow canal of the Morlacca, having the long, narrow island of Pago to our right, and the ancient Iapydia, the more modern Morlachia, to our left on the mainland. The Morlachs (who have thus given a name to the sea and shore), owing to their hitherto uncertain derivation, and the singular character of their customs, which resemble, in many respects, those of the Tartars, have occupied the attention of most Dalmatian travellers. Whatever may be their origin, they now speak a Slave dialect, and have many of the characteristics of that race. Professor Schafarik, however, himself a Slave, and a great authority as regards the antiquities of that wide-spread people, suggests that they may be, in part at least, the remains of the ancient Avares, who, under the Emperor Heraklius, rapidly overran, and were then as speedily dispossessed of Dalmatia by the Croats A.D. 630-40. He adds, that

as late as 949, in the days of Constantine
Porphyrogenitus, some of these Avares were
still apparent in Croatia, known, probably,
by their dress and dialect.   The title of
Ban or Bayan still exists in Persia, and is
of Avarish origin, though afterwards adopted
by the Servian princes of Bosnia in the
eleventh and twelfth centuries.   " Morlach "
is itself derived from the Slave language—
viz. from "more" = the sea, and "Vlach" = a
" Wallachian " or " Forlan " now-a-days, but
originally the designation of a Celt or Welsh-
man.   Modern Wallachians and Forlans are
of Italian origin.

The channel often grows so narrow as to
appear like a river, and not a wide one.   On
one side, the Croatian vines and olives are
cultivated in abundance; while on the other
—the island—runs a long, low cliff or bank,
on which no verdure grows.   The interior,
however, is not wanting in pastures and vines.
At the very narrowest, just before it turns
abruptly towards Zara, the ruins of a little

old fort remind one of the once insecure
state of this coast.   This and numerous other
small towers were built along the coasts of
the mainland and the islands after the marauding exploits of " Dragut," the famous Turkish pirate, and " Vruz Ali," pro-sultan of Tripoli, who swept off a multitude of Christians
for slavery from these coasts, many of whom
were ransomed by the Ragusans.   Neither
thus did this scourge cease.   Long afterwards
these narrow seas and sharp angles were the
lurking places of the Uskok corsairs, who were
strong enough when Sandys travelled to dispute
the seas with the Venetians, and, according
to the old English tourist, with success.   He
is sarcastic on the subject in his quaint way.
" The pirates hereabouts," says he, " do now
more than share with (the Venetians) in that
sovereignty, who gather such courage from
the timorousness of divers, that a little frigot
will often not fear to venture on an Argosie :*

* The etymology of Argosie is *not* from Argo, as Dr.
Johnson gives it, but from Ragusa.   "Ragosie," *i.e.* a Carack
from Ragusa.

nay, some of them will not abide the encoun-
ter, but run ashore before the pursuer (as if
a whale should flee from a dolphin), glad that
with wreck of ship and loss of goods they
may prolong a despised life, or retain unde-
served liberty !" This was of course before
the peace between Ferdinand and Venice
alluded to above, for Sandys travelled in
1610; but even at the end of the last century, the " citoyen Cassas," making the voyage
of Istria and Dalmatia to sketch the Roman
remains and most striking scenery for a
society of lovers of the beaux arts at Paris
and Vienna, ran, as M. Delavallee, his editor,
tells us, imminent danger near this very spot
from the same cause. Such perils are happily
now no more. It is to the credit of the Austrian marine that they have long since put
down all piracy in these parts. The Neverini
are less amenable, and, as the weather continued unsettled, I was not sorry to find
myself under cover of Zara as evening drew
on ; in default of romantic adventure success-

fully or unsuccessfully encountered, contented
to reflect on the exploits of the voyager in
ages past, who, besides the dangers of sea-
robbers, Uskok and Turk, Morlach and Sara-
cen, Norman and Narentan, had all the perils
of the elements in a narrow sea to contend
with, unmitigated by steam or even compass.

> "Illi robur et æs triplex
>   Circa pectus erat, qui fragilem truci]
> Commisit pelago ratem
>   Primus, nec timuit præcipitem Africum
> Decertantem Aquilonibus,*
>   Nec tristes Hyadas, nec rabiem Noti;
> Quo non arbiter Adriæ
>   Major tollere, seu ponere vult freta."

By six o'clock we were all safe ashore, and,
after the usual discipline of "Dogana" and
"Polizia," got inside the city gates and made
our way to our respective inns.

---

* The contests of the Scirocco, or south-west wind, with
the Bora, or north-east, "Notum," *or* "Africum Aquiloni-
bus," is a frequent phenomenon in the neighbourhood of the
Julian Alps and the northern shores of the Adriatic, nearly
always resulting in a fall of snow.

II.

DALMATIA—ST. JEROME—ZARA.

How much of all the complex interest we
feel in a place is summed up in its name!
The very look and sound of "Dalmatia" speak
of the past. It must surely be still the
Roman province, which we are approaching.
For Dalmatia, while it has so long borne the
same name, has no less long retained the same
character. It is always the " provincia" first
of Rome, then of Rome's eastern " alter
ego," Constantinople, then of Rome's eldest
daughter, Venice; and even now, though
temporal Rome has passed away, and Constantinople is Turkish, and Venice no more,
as if by a sort of destiny it hung to the last
vestige of the Roman name and power, it is
still the "province of the Römischer Kaiser,"

D

by which title the Emperor of Austria is to this day prayed for at Rome.

Yet Dalmatia first appears upon the page of history as forming part of a wide-spread independent kingdom. Of what race or language its former inhabitants were, as in the case of Istria, is enveloped in obscurity. Here, however, as there, the etymology of the ancient geographical names favours the theory of an early Slave population, which the most ancient writers* in that tongue tend to substantiate by laying claim to "Iljurik" or "Illyria," under which name Dalmatia is included. However it is also clear that great changes of inhabitants took place in these parts in very early times, and probable that after the invasion of Brennus and the Gauls (A.C. 360) considerable part of the peninsula lying between the Mediterranean and Euxine was occupied by Celts, while the race of the ancient, once widely extended Thracians, so ably

* Cf. Nestor, apud Schafariks Slawische Alterthümer, I. § 11, vol. i. 227.

described by the pen of Herodotus, shrank within the limits of the present Albanians or Arnauts, their conjectural descendants.

According to the Roman historians, about the time of the first Punic war Agron reigned over an " Illyrian " kingdom, which, including Istria to the north, and extending to Corfu southward, was powerful enough to hold its ground against the Macedonian successors of Alexander. On the death of Agron, and during the minority of her step-son Pinneus, Teuta, the late king's widow, held the reins of government, and came first into collision with the Romans. Her subjects, tempted doubtless by the character of their coast, after the manner of Dalmatians in more modern times, practised piracy, plundered the cargoes of the Italian merchants, captured their persons, and reduced them to slavery. Upon these grounds Rome stepped in and demanded redress. Queen Teuta, elated by her success in the war with the Greeks, not only refused it, but barbarianwise caused one of the Roman

ambassadors to be murdered after he had left
her palace. Invaded by sea and land at the
same time, her power fell in the first year of
the war, and, after the cession of some of her
most important islands and towns, including
Issa, Durazzo, and Corfu, Pinneus succeeded
to a diminished and tributary kingdom, while
Teuta was forced to abdicate, and confined
in the island of Pharos. Somewhile after this
came the fall of the Macedonian dynasty.
The Illyrians had been engaged in continual
hostilities with Macedon, and at one time had
held part of that country in subjection; but
now, as if by a sort of destiny, they entered
into an alliance with Perseus just in time to
share a like fate. One consul defeated and
took the Illyrian Gentius in his stronghold
of "Scodra," or Skutari, while the other
conquered and captured the Macedonian.
Fifty years after this, Cæcilius Metellus reduced Dalmatia formally to a Roman province,
and was rewarded for easy services with the
title of "Dalmaticus." He wintered at Salonæ,

where *fétes* and games were exhibited in honour of his presence. In the division of the Roman provinces made by Augustus between the Senate and himself, Dalmatia fell to the former, and in the latter years of this emperor it was the scene of a revolt under the chieftain Batho, which, through the coincidence of an insurrection in Pannonia, was formidable enough to shake Rome to its centre, and which nothing short of the policy of an Augustus, aided by the military talents of a Tiberius and Germanicus, could have successfully resisted. This war Suetonius calls the most serious of any since the Punic; and with it ended the last hopes of ancient Dalmatian independence. Henceforth it became one of the nurseries of the Roman fleets and armies. Several of its successful soldiers succeeded to the purple; two especially, both illustrious for their secular grandeur, both infamous as persecutors of the Christian Church; Decius and Diocletian. Diocletian was born and died there. He was born and derived his name from Dioclea, near Narona, or Narenta. He expired in his own vast pile on the sea-shore near Salonæ,—in his "palatium," which still remains a witness to the grand conceptions and boundless resources of its imperial designer.

Dalmatia is commonly reputed to have been the birthplace of St. Jerome; but the site of his native town is the subject of interminable dispute, and has in fact no fewer claimants than that of Homer. It might cause some disappointment to the traveller, who has got thus far, eager to find himself where the great doctor of the church first saw light, to learn that there is almost a concursus of writers, who have dedicated their learned labours to this subject, and one of whom has written a folio to prove his point, who place the "Natale Solum S. Hieronymi," not far from the confluence of the Mur and Drave, near Cilli, on the road from Laybach towards Vienna! Nor will he be much better pleased, I fear, when he hears that another folio overturns this hypothesis in favour of Stregna or Sdrigna, in Istria. Another authority, who would place it on the Kerka, in modern Dalmatia, would be—*here* at least—listened to with more gusto, if one could by any ingenuity make Skardona and Strydon the same names. A fourth removes it into Italy. A fifth says it was in Hungary. A sixth, that it is, to the best of his judgment, "nowhere;" and a recent French traveller, without pretending, to be sure, to much investigation, places it quietly in that "Haupt-Punkt" of interest to modern tourists, Spalatro itself, which, *if true,* would be a glorious termination to the inquiry : but unfortunately it rests hitherto on the assumption of M. Marnier.

Yet Dalmatia's claim to this honour relies on the words of a witness no less unexceptionable than St. Jerome himself, who, in his work on ecclesiastical writers, at his own name, says, "born of his father Eusebius, in the town of Strydon, which was formerly overthrown by the Goths, on the confines of

Dalmatia and Pannonia." This seems at first sight definite enough to preclude doubt, and in St. Jerome's own times no doubt it really was so; but unfortunately the terms "Pannonia" and "Dalmatia" are of all others in ancient history vague. Especially under the Roman emperors their limits were repeatedly altered, so that the name of Dalmatia is given to countries far beyond either its modern or more ancient range. Being then reduced to choose amongst opinions, and to avoid the appearance of adopting the sixth hypothesis, which would reduce St. Jerome to a myth, I will state what I have heard in those parts, or met with elsewhere, in favour of Stregna in Istria. The merit, however, of this claimant is nearly confined to its lying most within reach, and having been long under the jurisdiction of Aquileja, from which it is distant only about forty miles. Now it is certain that St. Jerome was connected with Aquileja in very early life. Somewhile in his youth he resided there, and, according to local tra-

dition at least, taught in its schools.*   Of its
clergy and religious he speaks in terms of
high eulogium in his epistles, and with its
learned he lived in close intimacy;—of which
we have an example in his friendship with
Rufinus.   Further, he committed his sister
to the care of some priests of that see,—
because, as he explains, there was no one in
his native town whom he could entrust with
such a charge,—and besought of them con-
solatory letters addressed to her from their
bishop.   All this seems at least to infer that
Strydon was not remote from Aquileja, probably that it was within its jurisdiction.
Now Stregna is within one day's journey, and
possesses a church, which tradition asserts to
have been originally raised over the tomb of
Eusebius.

The rest of the history of Dalmatia may
be thus shortly summed up :—After the division of the empire into East and West, it

* Written up over St. Jerome's chapel, in the old cathedral
church of Aquileja.

fell sometimes to the one, sometimes to the other. At the second division, however, after the death of Theodosius I., it belonged to the West from Honorius to Augustulus. Thence it passed into the hands of the Goths, until they in turn were overthrown by the generals of Justinian, and it thus became re-attached to Constantinople. Still exposed to the invasion of those fierce tribes, who overran the Roman world, we find it next resisting the Bulgares, but falling under the Huns and Avares, who besieged and took Salonæ. The Emperor Heraklius at that time wore the purple at Constantinople. Too much occupied with the incursions of the Saracens to be able to send any direct assistance to his vassals, he despatched messengers to the Croats, a Slave nation then dwelling on the Carpathian range, where Gallicia touches on Poland, and offered them the whole province provided they expelled his enemies, the Avares, and held it under his supremacy. Accordingly they came, A.D. 630, or thereabouts, after four years of combat finally subdued the Avares, and occupied the whole country, except those coast and island towns which were already, as we have seen; in the hands of friendly Italians, subject or closely allied to Constantinople. Such was the origin of those Slave kingdoms—for they were divided under different chiefs—which lasted until they were overthrown by the Turks in the fifteenth century, and with whom came the Illyrian language, the softest, and, in virtue of its adoption by the Ragusan writers, the most cultivated of the southern Slave dialects.

On this conquest hung the future fate of Dalmatia. The Croats were especially divided into two districts : * those who dwelt around Sziszek, including the country about Agram and Carlstadt, and most of what is now called Croatia ; and those about Belgrade, on the coast, extending also along the coast of Dalmatia, and conterminal with the Slaves of

* Cf. Schafarik's Slawische Alterthümer.

Bosnia, &c. Their rulers, uniting both districts, were called Bans of Croatia and Dalmatia. The seven Italian towns, mentioned
in a former letter, with the narrow territory
attached to each, had separate jurisdictions,
and formed henceforth all that remained of
the old Roman province.

It was this latter which Venice laid claim
to; and the Senate grounded its right on two
gifts, made, as they asserted, by the Emperors
Basil II., A.D. 975, and Alexius Comnenus,*
about a century later. They had, however,
formidable competitors in the Kings of Hungary. One of these, Caloman, the son of
Ladislaus, in 1102 conquered Croatia, and
then uniting with Venice to resist the Nor-
mans, whose piracies succeeded those of the
Saracens on these coasts, remained finally in
possession of Zara. Henceforth it became the
scene of a long struggle between the Hunga-
rians and Venetians. The doge styled himself
duke, the King of Hungary king of Dalmatia,

---

* Died A.D. 1118.

while a third party arose among the Slave princes, who, about 1250, appear to have had the advantage. In the next century, however, Charles, or Charobert, having put an end to the pretensions of the Slaves, his son-in-law (A.D. 1381) quite expelled the Venetians, and obliged the doge to renounce his title of duke. Notwithstanding which, again, shortly after, their successor, Ladislas, struggling with Charles of Anjou for Naples, sold Zara and Dalmatia to the Venetians for 100,000 ducats, by which means the republic eventually recovered all its possessions, and thenceforth could by no efforts of Turk or Hungarian be dispossessed. Finally, on the dismemberment of the States of Venice at the treaty of Campo Formio, it was apportioned to Austria, 1797.

It was almost night by then we were out of the hands of a very rigorous set of custom-house officers, and fairly within the walls of Zara. Here I was informed that the next steamer for Spalato and Ragusa would not leave until Thursday morning. Accordingly, having speedily explored the ramparts, which are quite specimens of the magnificent architectural notions of Venice, in this respect especially worthy of her Roman lineage, early on the following morning I commenced upon the town. At once it recalls to mind Venice. The same courts, with wells for rain-water in the centre; the same comparatively lofty houses, and narrow streets for *foot*-passengers only; the same piazza, on a reduced scale, with its hall of justice, its church, even its *cafés;* the same Oriental marble columns scattered about; the bell-towers; the Byzantine churches, dedicated to saints not only of the New but also of the Old Testament; and the same favourite French improvement of modern days, "public gardens," in front of which are some excellent and very handsome stone wells of spring water, the greatest boon, probably, bestowed by the nineteenth century on ancient "Jadera." I went into the church of St. Simeon the prophet, whose entire body is said to be here preserved in a magnificent silver sarcophagus behind the high altar, supported on angels, which were once likewise of the same precious metal, until the Municipium on some occasion sold them, and substituted a baser metal. The body was exposed to view through a crystal, or, as some assert, Venetian glass window, to public veneration at a particular hour every day during the solemnization of the festival, which was then going on, but I had not the fortune to arrive at the right time to see it. Large pictures, after the Venetian schools of art, describe the legend of Queen Elizabeth of Hungary, who was the donor of the sarcophagus. Zara was then under Hungarian rule, and she came there to venerate the body of St. Simeon, which was accordingly exposed before her. Suddenly the idea seized her of appropriating one of the fingers, which she accordingly broke off the dry but otherwise perfectly preserved hand, and hastily concealed in her bosom. Instantly it became full of worms, and the queen fainted with horror. When she was sufficiently recovered, acknowledging her error, she reverently replaced it upon the hand, to which it adhered as naturally as though it had never been removed. The silver coffin, &c. was her gift, as an offering of expiation for what she had once dared to attempt. Another miracle, in more modern times, is also related to have taken place at this shrine when the French were in possession, in the days of Napoleon I. The object of the thief, however, on this occasion, was simply plunder. A party of French soldiers had been despatched under an officer, by the commandant, to bring away the precious metal. The officer made two attempts; first, he was seized with a universal tremor: the second time, his arm was struck with paralysis. On this, he prudently desisted from the enterprise, and presently recovered. St. Simeon is the patron saint, or, as they call it, "gonfaloniero," of Zara.

The interior of the church was fine, and glittering after Dalmatian fashion for the festival. The dresses of the people were certainly not less ornamental. The men often exhibited the old Austrian pigtail, tied with ribbon, appearing from beneath a red or black and gold-embroidered and tasselled cap, their loose trousers blue, with red edgings, and a red waistcoat, with jacket slung on hussar fashion. The women's heads were covered with white kerchiefs, bordered with a red stripe or hem, thrown loosely on; and they wore purple polkas trimmed with red, purple "krilo" or petticoat, and their *opankès* laced with scarlet. All the peasantry on this coast, from Fiume inclusive, wear, not shoes, but the *opankè*, which is made of a sort of untanned (but otherwise prepared) hide, tied on with thongs, the sole projecting beyond the foot, and admirably suited to protect it on these stony hills.

As already hinted, the town was splendidly fortified by the Venetians, and served as a sort of breakwater to the tide of Turkish marauders, who, from the reign of Mahomet II., ravaged Bosnia and Dalmatia. It is interesting to see how the history of the place is built

E

into its walls and public buildings.   Here the
gate towards the sea exhibits portions of a
Roman triumphal arch (dedicated by a wife to
her husband, like the "Porta Aurea" at Pola),
of which the architect in the. middle ages has,
as in Istria, availed himself for his portal.   In
St. Simeon's, we find the silver sarcophagus of
Queen Elizabeth, described above.   Elsewhere,
an isolated, lantern-like tower rises into the
sky, in which tradition says that "Boro
d' Antoni," a king's son, was in mythical ages
starved to death.   As one passes out by
the gate towards the external fort, another
handsome and new-looking gate, of solid stone
masonry, relates of itself that it was erected in
1543, to complete the fortifications of this
capital of Dalmatia.   The recently-made wells,
the public gardens, speak of Austrian and
French rule; while, external to the city, the
ruins of an old acqueduct, leading no one can
tell *whither*, but certainly to a great distance,
inform the amateur of classic remains, that the
water, so much needed in later centuries, was

brought into the city, at whatever cost, by Roman magnificence.

Zara is now the provincial Austrian seat of government, and is said to contain 2,000 *employés* in a population of five or six thousand. Just outside the town is a village of Catholic Arnauts, who emigrated hither many years since to escape Turkish rule and misrule: no uncommon spectacle on this coast since the fifteenth century. A similar village of Greek Slaves may be seen at Peroj in Istria; in both cases they retain their national dress and language.

I had a letter of introduction to the Consigliere Marchesani, with whom I spent the rest of my time at Zara, and from whom, besides much useful information, I received letters of recommendation for my onward journey.

III.

THE next morning, when I got on board,
all things were changed.   The "Barone
Kübeck" had given way to the "Istria;" the
young, good-natured captain, who brought us
from Fiume, was replaced by another, not
wanting in politeness, but a middle-aged
man, who had a wife and children.   The
passengers were also changed, and become
much more numerous.   In the first place,
there was a detachment of soldiers, and the
officers thereto.   Secondly, two Greek priests,
and one of them, by his dress and the cross
hanging from his neck, obviously a dignitary.
Thirdly, two Italians from Verona or Brescia,
one of whom, wearing black "tights" and a

broad-brimmed white hat, I thought had
much the appearance of an American citizen
from the southern States, until I was assured,
on unquestionable authority, that he was
a Lombard priest, travelling " *incognito.*"
Fourthly, a drawing-master in the Government
school of design at Cattaro, to whose polite
attentions M. de Marchesani had recommended me; and, fifthly, an elderly Austrian
captain of artillery, who, having been long
stationed in Lyssa, was on the move to more
roomy quarters. Gradually we all grew acquainted with one another. The Lombards
were bound, like myself, for Montenegro, with
a fell determination, which they certainly
did not act up to, of seeing everything
worth seeing on the road thither. They
had the merit of breaking the ice with the
Greek dignitary, who was rather an awful
personage, and to the future career of some
of us, as the event proved, not a little important. He was a strikingly handsome
man, full six feet tall, and, perhaps, thirty

years of age, with a fair complexion, light-
orown hair, Vandyke beard and moustache,
slightly acquiline features, which his lofty
cap, and the red and purple of his priest's
dress, helped much to set off. His companion had the air of extreme youth, and, in
fact, was only just in deacon's orders. He
also wore the common Greek ecclesiastical
dress, which is blue or light purple. I
found they were coming from Segna, where
there is a Greek college, and going to Montenegro, not, however, on a visit, but for a
permanency. Since the alteration introduced
there through the instrumentality of the
Cabinet at St. Petersburgh on the death of
the late Vladika, whereby the primitive episcopal government has been changed into the
more ordinary form of a principality, there
has been no ecclesiastical dignitary there : a
want which this "archimandrite" (Greek for
abbé) was going to supply. He was very
civil, and made the proposal that we should
all travel on together from Cataro to Cettinja,

which, not foreseeing future impediments, I willingly assented to.

After this I went and had some conversation with the Austrian military, whom I found very cross on the subject of the (*then*) impending war. They thought, or pretended to think, it less injurious to Austrian interests that the Principalities should remain in the hands of the Russians, the mouth of the Danube be closed to commerce, and the Black Sea a Russian lake, than that England, and "my Lord Palmerston's agents," should become their permanent neighbours in Turkey. Neither would they be persuaded, they said, with British India before their eyes, and the *quondam* French colonies in various parts of the world, and the Ionian Islands at their own door, and the desirable Egypt beyond, that Great Britain had other than designs admirable for her own advantage, to be sure, but somewhat detrimental to her neighbours. So I soon left off talking politics, and abandoned these perverse people to their own conceits with a .... "tempus monstrabit!" The captain told me that the fortifications made by the English at Lyssa— for it was fortified against the French in the late war—were very strong, independent of more recent Austrian works. Especially, it was the former who introduced that natural chevaux de frise, the Aloe—"Agave Americana"—whose sharp, prickly leaves are very difficult to pass, and even dangerous to the too adventurous intruder.

As we completed a long channel between the low, stony hills of an island on one side and those of the mainland on the other, scantily clothed with the olive and the vine, we wound into a bay under a splendid fort of massive granite, looking so fresh it might have been finished last year, though in truth one of the noble works erected on this coast as a protection against the Turks, by Sammicheli, for the Signoria of Venice, three hundred years ago. A few minutes more, and we were within eye-shot of our next sleeping-place. The effect of winding into the broad lagoon, or harbour, was very happy. At first, on looking towards the shore for Sebeniko, no houses appeared: nothing but the eternal grey rocks. All at once, a town seemed to spring up from the earth, and what we had taken for stones, &c., grew into churches, houses, quays, streets; doors and windows instinct with life. The town, which Fortis calls "the best placed and best inhabited after Zara of any city in Dalmatia," is of the indigenous stone, and, at a little distance, appears a mere continuation of the rocky coast. There is nothing in it worth seeing, except the Cathedral, a work of the *renaissance*, and about four hundred years old. This appears to have been executed by Byzantine artists, and is quite a gem of its style. It is of white limestone, the roof being supported on a double row of Grecian columns, connected with round arches; and everything throughout on a like scale of magnificence and beauty. The high altar is at the top of

two flights, the first of six, the second of
eight or ten steps; being thus admirably
adapted for the more imposing ceremonials.
The roof is arched; it has clerestory windows,
and two aisles. The whole building, as far
as I could judge by the eye, is not very
large, contrasted with the great churches of
Venice, for instance; but it struck me—for
I saw it best on my return—what a contrast
in regard of strength and durability it presented to the Roman buildings on the same
coast. Here, a church, originally of great
expense and splendour, endowed with funds
for its repair, and in continual use, yet re-
quiring fundamental restoration after the lapse
of four centuries, to prevent it from falling
down. At Pola and Spalato are temples,
arches, and amphitheatres, which, with every
disadvantage of lead and iron cramps removed, windows and doors pierced where they
were not, according to the original design,
intended; uninhabited, dismantled, abandoned
to the destructive influence of the elements;

yet, at the end of fifteen hundred years, standing still, towers of strength, in little less than their pristine glory, and bidding fair, unless removed, ever to stand, monuments of the greatest earthly magnificence, to the very end of time!

It was not, however, until my return that I had time to go over this duomo, having beforehand concerted with my friend the drawing-master a scheme for viewing the Falls of the Kerka, which, he thought, would bring me there by half-past five P.M.; thus allowing the last hour of daylight to see this most picturesque cataract. But, alas! though we arrived off Sebenik at half after two, it was *four* before we were set on shore, had passed the *polizia* and *dogana*, and threaded our way through a narrow street— five minutes' walk—to the inn. Such is the state of travelling in Austria in the middle of the nineteenth century! We were standing amongst a knot of passengers and townspeople at the door of the inn, which is in the midst

of the steep ascent whereon the town is
built, when he communicated this disheart-
ening advice. As I was reflecting on the
aggravated mishap of losing the Kerka Falls,
and having to spend the whole afternoon and
evening with nothing to do at Sebenik, which
had a remarkably unpromising look about it,
I suddenly bethought myself, that what could
not be seen by sunlight might yet be visible,
and even beautiful, by light of moon; and
that, at any rate, a good walk across the
country during the remaining hour and half
of daylight would be refreshing and interesting.   At once, I communicate my thought
to the innkeeper, and he, with ready wit, to a
Dalmatian youth standing hard-by, whose middle height and brawny limbs were concealed or
adorned with red cap, brown hussar jacket
slung across his shoulders, with blue trousers,
laced with yellow down his legs, and terminat-
ing somewhat short of the usual *opankè*. He
was quite the man for a walk, and, of course,
knew the shortest way across the hills. A

bargain was soon effected. It was in vain
my steamer friends remonstrated and pro-
phesied ill of the expedition, predicting that,
if I were not stopped and robbed on the
road, I should assuredly see nothing of the
falls, and, quite as certainly, be too late to
proceed with the steamer next morning. We
could not agree, and I made haste to depart.
My guide, animated by the discussion, of
which he did not understand one word, but
of which he learned the drift from his friend
the innkeeper, snatched the dirk (which, in
Dalmatia, most of the peasantry carry, having,
until lately, borne firearms also, like the
Turks and Montenegrins) out of the girdle
of his next neighbour, and stuck it into his
own, while I brandished my walking-stick,
and away we went in a fierce spirit of resolution, as fast as ever our legs could carry
us. The road lay first up the stony hills,
on foot of which Sebenïk stands. Then,
bending to the left across the fields, it continued along an unmacadamized footpath,

strewed with stones so hard, and rough, and angular, that the stoutest nail-shod shooting-shoes were a poor protection. Here the advantage of the *opankè*, which my guide wore, was manifest. Not only does the untanned hide yield less to the constant hammering, and so afford a more effectual armour to the sole, but, by its excess of width, allows the foot to expand naturally at each step, and wards off sharp corners from the more yielding texture which forms the covering of the foot. Away we went, faster and faster, as the sun sank lower and lower, across fields, tenanted now and then by a few black and white horned sheep, whose fleece inclined rather to hair than wool; over rough banks, covered with low firs and junipers, with here and there a little cultivation, chiefly vines and the *maraska,—i.e.*, a kind of cherry of which the liqueur maraschino is made at Zara.

The last rays of the sun were falling horizontally upon us, as its "golden corse" sank beneath the blue waters of the Adriatic, when, at the bottom of a steep path, leading through a rugged and narrow gully, we found ourselves on the shore of an inland sea-water lake, or rather *embouchure* of the river Kerka, and sat down to wait for the ferry. To the left, through a narrow Bosphorus, the water found its way out into a second similar lake whence it finally emerged into the fine harbour of Sebenik. To the right rolled slowly along the deep flood of the Kerka, as wide, perhaps, as the Thames above London; while opposite, the last gleam of the setting sun drew one's attention to the middle-age city of Skardona, lying on a little promontory, stretching into the lake. This was not the site of the more ancient city. That stood on the shores of the outer estuary, called Proclia, where I was told Cyclopean ruins were still to be discovered in serene weather, below the water-level. Behind the more modern town rise two rugged-looking castles, of the rudest construction. This country abounds in such, and it appears, by contemporary documents,

—so I was told by the well-informed Pretor of Skardona—they were raised by the peasants, like the Tabors of Carniola, at the time of the first Turkish marauding incursions. They are provided neither with doors nor windows, but are entered by means of a ladder, at a sort of square opening on the first or second floor, which thus serves instead of gate and drawbridge; the ladder being drawn up after the entrance of the garrison. The same sort of entrance existed formerly at the old castle of Luegg, in Carniola, between Trieste and Laibach; and another is still visible and ready for use at Cetinja, in Montenegro. As a means of personal protection, they were more or less available; but they could not protect the lands around, which were ravaged and destroyed by the Turks, who only suffered these castles to escape when there was nothing within them to compensate for the trouble and loss of a siege.

The sound of the Angelus bell came " soft and silvery" across the water, and the deepening shadows of evening advanced apace as we seated ourselves, somewhat less fresh than when we left Sebenik, upon some great stones by the water's edge, awaiting the advent of the ferry-boat; of which at present there were no traces visible on the opposite side—about a mile distant. A group of girls and women, in their pretty characteristic dresses, had come up and were waiting, like ourselves, to get across; while, close to the shore on our left, a man in a boat with a shoulder-of-mutton sail, was filling a hogshead from skins of wine, which three or four asses had brought to this, their place of embarkation for Skardona. He offered us a cup, which we accepted with gratitude, after a walk of ten miles under a broiling sun, and found it an excellent sort of red " Maraschina," which bore witness to the fact that a rocky soil does not injure the quality of wine. Thus the stony Carst about Trieste produces the famed " Prosecco; " the rocks around Sebenik and Spalato, Maraschina; Ragusa is the habitat of Malmsey, &c., &c., &c.

F

We had a droll scene when the boat did come at last; for it proved to be a very small one, and there were abundance of men, women, and donkeys, all to be ferried over in it at once. However, we each got in according to the orders of the ferryman: first, myself and guide, then the women, then the donkeys, and lastly the men—having first shoved us off. As to the asses, they strongly objected to sharing the dangers of the deep, until they were hauled in tumultuously by the tails and ears; all lending a hand, amidst deafening shouts of laughter.

When we had reached the landing-place I went up straight to the " Pretorium," having a letter from head-quarters, *i.e.*, Zara, to the Pretor, as he is called. Now, I should premise that, after leaving Sebenik, no one was to be met with who could speak any language but Dalmatian, that is, Slave. German was quite unknown, and a few words of Italian the utmost one ever met with; hence the reader may judge of my surprise when the Pretor, a gentleman about thirty, and not at first distinguishable from any ordinary Austrian *employé*, after reading my letter, addressed me fluently in English! He had learned, he said, nearly twelve years ago at Vienna; and though, during an eight or ten years' residence in these parts, he had very, very rarely met with any opportunity of practising it, was still quite *au fait* at doing so, whenever an occasion did present itself. I found in him an intelligent and agreeable companion who at once entered into my moonlight scheme, and made all necessary arrangements for me. The falls were an hour distant up the Kerka, and it was already twilight; in the morning I must be off in the gray unless I meant to lose my place in the steamer, and my reputation with its company. So we engaged a four-oared cutter to be in attendance, and as soon as night was fairly set in, *i.e.*, about half-past seven, started for the falls, he kindly leaving some fifty letters—the unhappy fate of Austrian *employés*—to be written, instead of sleeping on his return.

The moon was brightening as we left Skardona; it was already brilliant at our arrival
beneath the falls; and, when we reached the
heights above, shed magnificently its pale but
clear light over the whole expanse of foam and
spray, as it leapt down a hundred different
cascades, over rocks, through trees and
wooded islands, in an ample crescent to the
loamy level below. Reckoning in the whole
of its subdivisions, it must be considerably
wider than the Rhine at Schaffhausen; unless,
indeed, I were deceived by the moon's poetic
rays. The effect was lovely; and I had every
reason to be contented that I had persevered
in the resolution of coming on from Sebenik;
though there is little doubt that it would be
yet more beautiful by daylight, enriched as it
must then be by all the thousand colours
of the surrounding landscape.

The rocks around are of tupha. There is
no grand, deep fall of water, but a multitude
of small, successive cascades, which *en masse*
create a deafening roar, to be heard a mile or

two from the spot. The islands, formed by the rocks overgrown with wood, are quite inaccessible, except by chance during a few days in *very* warm, dry summers, such as do not ordinarily occur above once in many years. Hence, a little while since, the centre and largest was overrun with wild goats. A pair, supposed to be in bad health, were left there purposely one of these extraordinary dry seasons. So well did the "watering-place" agree with the invalids, that they not only throve themselves, but left a numerous and increasing progeny, who thus lived separated from the rest of the world, and safe for many years from the intrigues of the tyrant biped, who ruled all around. One unfortunate day,—last summer, I believe,—their enemies, not without risk to themselves, again got upon the island, and they were all killed down, and once more reduced to a single pair.

The stream carried us back to Skardona much quicker than we came; and, after supper and some conversation about the neighbourhood with the hospitable Pretor, I retired for a few hours to rest. Before dawn I had bidden him adieu, and was again on my road to Sebenik. Though we started, as it seemed, judging by how long it had taken us to come the evening before, in ample time, I was now astonished to find how far it was to return; having more ascent, and being still somewhat the worse, perhaps, for yesterday's rapid walk. It approached the hour for the steamer's departure, and we were still at a distance. We hurried on, climbed the steep ascents, and rushed down the corresponding declivities; at length we gained the last hill, and looked eagerly down into the harbour, to see if there were still any hopes. To my joy, there lay the steamer puffing and panting, and, in short, just getting up her steam. All were on board, already they had weighed anchor, the wheels began to move, the hawser sped over the gunwale, the vessel trembled convulsively, when I sprang triumphantly across the narrow plank, and was received by all my companions

—Italians, Slaves, Greeks, and Germans, who had quite given me over, but were now drawn up upon the quarter-deck, ready to cast a last look on Sebenik, with a hearty cheer!

The voyage to Spalato occupied five hours, through the same style of scenery as before, that is to say, between barren-looking, rocky islands and mountainous coast, sometimes sprinkled with vines and olives, or more thickly clad with the low fir and juniper, with here and there a little town—its fortifications stamped with the lion of St. Mark's. All these towns were fortified by the Venetians, who also built the streets narrow for the sake of defence, like those of the parent city; for it will be remembered that in the early days of the republic they owed their safety to the defeat of the Huns and other enemies in their narrow lagunes. This feature is a characteristic also of the towns on the coast of Istria.

We turned to the left round the island of Bua, across which, partly on the mainland,

and partly in the island, lies the town called
Trau, the "Tragurium" of Pliny,* "marmore
notum," and united to Salonæ by the celebrated "Via dei Castelli." Fortis calls attention to it, not only for its mineral productions—amongst which is the "pissalphalt,"
used anciently by the Egyptians for embalm-
ing their dead, but also as possessing a date
palm, which bore abundance, though not the
finest quality of fruit. "Its climate," he says,
"is beautiful, and productive of oil, wine,
figs, and almonds; but also of the 'Pauk,'
a venomous spider,—like the Tarantula in
Puglia,—the remedy for whose bite is analogous to that in use in Southern Italy, and
consists in swinging five or six hours on the
slack-rope."

Bua was used as a place of banishment by
the later emperors. The heretic Jovinian, for
example, was sent here by Honorius.

---

* According to Fortis there are some ruins not far off
called Trau Vecchio, on the site, as it was once supposed, of
the Roman city; but in fact only *medieval* buildings, raised
after the introduction of Christianity.

A little further, at the bottom of a small bay forming its harbour, Spalato, *olim* Spolatum, and the "Palatium" of Diocletian, comes into sight. It lies on a promontory, the other side of which forms the estuary, on which Salonæ stood. The modern town, containing about 12,000 souls, covers an area somewhat less than the double of that on which the ruins of the ancient palace stand. Hence, when we remember how large a space is now rendered unavailable by ruined arches, temples, and the *débris* of houses, we shall arrive at some idea of the size of this once vast palace. As in the case of the amphitheatre at Pola, one sees its elevation from the sea before landing ; that is to say, its *present* elevation ; the *original* elevation one does *not* see, for the front of the palace was raised on arches, now subterranean, in order to level the foreground with the rise behind it. On a plane with the top of these arches, is at present a stone pavement, running along the quay. From this level arise fifty marble columns, forming the ancient façade of the palace towards the sea. These columns were originally distinct, but have been in more modern times united with masonry, to form the walls of the middle-age town, which lay wholly within the palace. Since that, they have been again pierced, above, with the windows of dwelling-houses, beneath, with the doors of numerous shops. It is not difficult, and well worth while, to descend into the warehouse of one of these latter to see the stupendous solidity on which the upper fabric rests. In figure the palace was an equilateral parallelogram, having four gates opposite one another, each in the centre of its respective side. On the side we have been speaking of is the Porta Argentea, or Marine Gate; opposite, toward Salonæ, but not yet excavated, the Porta Aurea; to the left, the Porta Ferrea; to the right, the Porta Ænea.

Entering now through the Porta Argentea, one passes along an arched, and soon, owing to the hill at the back, *underground* passage.

Turning out of this to the left, a flight of steps becomes visible, leading up into a circular building, by some called the Vestibule, by others thought to have been one of the four temples which formed the nucleus of the palace. If instead of ascending the stairs you pursue the path which you were in before, you come to the remains of the private or palatial amphitheatre, small indeed compared with those of Pola, Verona, or Salonæ, yet sufficiently vast to find within the walls of a single palace! *Within* the round temple or vestibule, already mentioned, one of its doorways is highly ornamented, and leads beneath a colonnade into the "Forecourt" of the palace, now called the "Piazza del Duomo." The opposite doorway, and indeed the whole side, is gone, but it was probably once the approach to the State or Imperial apartments, overlooking the harbour and sea. Following the first-mentioned doorway into the Piazza, one finds it still surrounded by its ancient portico, the pillars of which are of granite,

finished with Corinthian capitals, from which
spring the arches which support the archi-
trave.   On the left side—as one stands looking towards the Vestibule—is the Temple
(said to have been) of Jupiter, now the
Cathedral, while opposite on the right hand
is that of Æsculapius, now the Baptistery.
The former—*i.e.* the Duomo—is an octagonal
building, surrounded by a Roman peristyle,
supporting a gallery formed of huge flat
stones, resting against the outside of the
dome, and wide enough for several people to
walk abreast around it.   This temple rests
upon columns and arches of the same gigantic
proportions.   Inside are eight granite columns, surmounted by the like number of
granite and porphyry mixed, of smaller size,
above which rises the dome, or cupola.   This
is built internally of bricks arranged *in successive arches*, which intersect one another,
and is a method of building well known to
the Romans, as calculated greatly to increase
the strength of the whole.   Externally it is

formed of massive quadrate stones, laid close to one another, each fitting into its place without any cement, but riveted together with iron cramps leaded into each block,—truly the conception of an architect who was building for future millenaries! On mounting into the first gallery inside—for there are two—one perceives a variety of friezes representing the chase, which has given rise to the notion that this temple was originally dedicated, not to Jupiter, but Diana. In the second gallery the wall acts as a conductor to the voice, and the slightest whisper is heard all round, just as in the " Whispering Gallery" at St. Paul's, London.

Opposite the cathedral stands the Baptistery or temple of Æsculapius, smaller than the last, but scarcely less magnifical. It is constructed of even yet more massive slabs than the last; without a peristyle; its ceiling of white marble finely groined. On the top has been placed —to the horror of the antiquarian—by some medieval architect, a square campanile, or bell-tower. One may, however, easily imagine it away, for the point of union between the original building and the later addition is sufficiently obvious. And one can hardly regret the striking monument thus formed, by the surmounting of the heathen temple with the Christian bell-tower, of that greatest revolution which the world has ever seen!

There are a variety of minor objects of interest scattered about, as, *e. g.*, a stone representing the battle of the Centaurs and Lapithæ in the Seminary; another of the Passage of the Red Sea, of inferior workmanship, supposed to belong to the times of Theodosius, in a church; also a number of glass sepulchral urns, lacrymatories, signets, vases, and earthenware lamps with figures of animals well executed on them, collected together into a small museum—all of which will to some extent reward the diligent investigator of Roman antiquities.

But, although it was most convenient to describe the remains of Diocletian's palace,

&c. in this letter, it was not on this occasion that I found opportunity of examining them. Amongst the advantages to the tourist of making the voyage of Dalmatia in Lloyd's boats is that, passing over the same ground twice in going and returning, he pays a double visit to the towns of most interest, and can thus reserve what he has not time to see properly for his return. Leaving, therefore, Spalato for the present, I joined the Lombards in hiring a carriage to go to the ruins of Salonæ, two or three miles distant, recently excavated under the superintendence of Professor Carrara, a native of this place, though ordinarily engaged in the Museum at Venice.

The day was fine. The first indication of the proximity of one of the more important towns of the Roman empire appears in the arches of an aqueduct, which one sees in the fields to the right within a mile above Spalato. A very small portion of it remains : enough to show that the Romans never neglected to procure a copious supply of the best water in the neighbourhood. A mile or two further, on a gentle half-moon slope, looking towards Spalato, is the site of Salonæ, traced out by the remains of the city wall, much of which is in good preservation. It was defended by strong square towers, and pierced by as many as four or five gates, some of which still show the deep tracks of the chariot-wheels in their worn stones.* The convexity of the half-moon is turned from Spalato, and runs along the highest part of the rise on which the town stood. Thence the ground shelves gradually down to a road leading to the Via dei Castelli, and lying along the bank of a sedgy river, once probably kept clearer and more open to the sea, which it enters just below. At the lower line of the city on this waterside are some Cyclopean remains, which we passed on our way to the Castelli, but had neither time nor light

---

* Cæsar, in the 3d book of his "Bellum Civile," where he relates its obstinate and successful resistance of Octavius, describes it as "oppidum et loci naturâ et colle munitum." On this occasion they set all their slaves free, and used the women's hair to make warlike engines.

to examine more closely. The area between the road and the convexity at the top of the bank, now partly cultivated, partly excavated, and the rest rough, shrubby waste land, was occupied by the city, and would be, according to my eye, about half a mile across. In this space some baths and other public buildings have been made out. Another aqueduct, or, not improbably, an extension of that already mentioned, though at the extreme opposite end of Salonæ, seems to have conveyed water to the amphitheatre just without the largest gate, viz., that leading towards Bua. The walls of this aqueduct are covered with petrifactions, deposited when, first getting out of repair, the water trickled down the sides from the broken pipe or channel.

Some peasants followed us offering us Roman coins, silver and copper, of small intrinsic value, but which they professed to have found on the spot. Of three taken at hazard from a great many, one was inscribed with the name of *" Maximin. Pius. Aug. Germanicus "* over his head or effigy crowned with laurel, with *Fides Militum* around a female figure on the reverse. Another appears to be a coin of Constantius, the son of Constantine the Great; the third, of Arcadius, with s. M. K. underneath, "*signata moneta Karthagine*," in token of its having been coined at Carthage.

Salonæ suffered various sieges : twice from the Romans, by whom, in the fourth century, it was taken after a heroic resistance; twice in the seventh, when it fell never to rise again, being first taken and sacked by the Avares, and then, shortly after, a second time by the Slaves, who came to drive them out. The inhabitants migrated to Spalato and Ragusa, leaving Salonæ in the hands of the poorer Contadini, or peasants. After such vicissitudes, it is not likely to contain much of value.

The evening was drawing in as we drove along the Via dei Castelli towards Trau. These castles, of which there are seven, stand on the edge of the sea, and are said to have been built in the sixteenth century by Venetian nobles, as a protection to the cultivators of their estates from Turkish invaders. We stopped at the central one, which is also the largest, and called "Vittori." It is a solidly built, lofty, square edifice, and when, as once, surrounded by the sea, would have been a strong fortress, especially for those days.

IV.

RAGUSA.

EARLY the next morning, after a hot, disagreeable night on board, in closely-packed berths, we prosecuted our voyage; neither the remembrance of the past, nor the prospect of the future, nor the state of the present, being rendered more *couleur de rose*, but much the reverse, by the decided Sirocco which prevailed, and kept a head-wind before us the whole day. However, though not agreeable to thorough landsmen, it affected the sea very little until quite evening. The reason of this lay in the succession of island breakwaters by which one was defended. First, we ran along the "Canale di Brazza," until we reached Makarska, where the steamer remained an hour or two to lade and unlade. Thence we

emerged by means of the " Canale di Lessina,"
and then, retrograding somewhat through the
"Canale di Marenta," found our way to
" Curzola," where we repeated the same
operation as at Makarska, and then, as the
evening drew on, coasted along Meleda,—the
scene of St. Paul's shipwreck (commonly reputed at Malta), if the talented Ragusan
Giorgi, of the early part of the last century,
and the English commentator Bryant, might
be believed,—and, as it grew dark, got out of
all shelter and into rough water, to the · discomfiture of several and the discomfort of all.

Up to this period the time passed pleasantly
enough. Amongst others, I found the captain
intelligent and well informed, as are most
of the Austrian-Lloyd's officers. He praised
the Dalmatians, and said Lloyd's service, like
the Venetian navy of old, depended on them.
They have much capacity for everything, but
especially languages and navigation ; hence
they readily enter into foreign naval services,
and, in like manner as the Istrians, escape

the dreaded conscription by making voyages to America. They are also very faithful to their employers, and never revolted (latterly, at least) against their Venetian lords. The Ragusan fleet was manned by the same race, and bore a high reputation in the days of Charles V. and his Spanish successors. The Admiral of the Republic resided on the Isola di Mezzo, where his family still remain, retaining the hereditary title and *dress* of their ancestor, who served Charles in his wars, and was once honoured by receiving his handkerchief, an heirloom which is still in their possession. That of Admiral was the only office of importance in the State which did not go amongst the patricians; it was essentially civic, and confined to the members of that order.

Those numerous old castles which one sees on the islands all down the Gulf, however valuable once in troublous times, are now to be had cheap enough. There was one sold the other day by the municipality to which it belonged for ten pounds! The materials alone, had it been elsewhere, would have fetched five hundred pounds, they said; but it was situated on a barren, inaccessible rock, destitute of water.

As the evening advanced, the Sirocco increased, and, to add to our miseries on deck, it began to rain. Yielding, therefore, to necessity, I retreated into the cabin, laid myself up on a sofa, and was soon asleep. About midnight I was awoke from my somewhat uneasy slumbers by a change for the better. All was now tranquil; we had reached, and were presently moored in, the still harbour of Gravosa, there to pass the remainder of the night, ready to advance upon Ragusa the following morning.

As soon as ever it was light I was on deck, impatient to get ashore and contemplate the scene of the last of the middle-age republics; the little free state, which boasted Cadmus and Hermione as its progenitors, the Lacedemonians as its founders, the Romans as its colonists; which counted Greek emperors, Slave bans, Norman dukes, Hungarian kings, Spanish potentates, Turkish sultans at different epochs, the popes always as its protectors; the parent of Gondola, Palmotta, and Giorgi; the fosterer of a school of Latin, Italian, and Slave writers, which flourished through four or five centuries; the scene of the fatal earthquake in the seventeenth century; the oligarchical republic, whose protracted history is epitomised in its four names, Epidaurus of the Grecks and Romans, Rausium of the Byzantines, Dubrownik of the Slaves, and Ragusa of all the rest, in more modern times; which retained its own form of government from its earliest days quite into the nineteenth century, and some years beyond the term allotted to its powerful Venetian rival, surrendering at last to the gigantic power of Napoleon I., after so many centuries of independence.

There was nothing of any interest on the shore at Gravosa, but a Customs chamber

and a cabaret. At the former I deposited
all my dispensable luggage, to remain there
until I should return to reclaim it on the
road home. To the latter I went for a guide,
or rather to inquire if *without a guide* it
were possible for a person to lose his way to
Ragusa? It was *not* possible; so I set off
to the town, half an hour distant. A good
macadamized and gravelled carriage-road led
up the steep hill, or hogsback, of the promontory lying between Gravosa and Ragusa.
The fields on either side, though after so dry
an autumn, were quite green, and not only
the vine and olive, but, near the town, the
pomegranate was flourishing in full blow with
its rich scarlet flowers. Somewhere I passed
a Greek chapel on the road-side; and, on the
top of the ascent, got a full view of the
whole green oasis amongst rocks, in which
"Dubrownik" (so called, apparently, in reference to the wild spot on which it was
originally founded) stands, studded with little
white villas in gardens, not unlike English

cottages at Deal or Dover or Broadstairs, but all detached, and four out of five untenanted, and apparently dismantled by fire !

" Why, you seem to have suffered much from incendiaries here," said I to a Ragusan fellow-traveller, whom I overtook just as he had struggled up the hill, on the top.

" That, signore," said he, " was the work of the Allies in the last war—the Russians, the Montenegrins, and the English."

" Gl' Inglesi ! " exclaimed I—for all the educated classes here, as in the rest of the towns on this coast, speak Italian.

" Si, signore, and the Inglesi were the worst of the three, for they prevented our houses from ever being rebuilt."

And so indeed it was. Napoleon, as it will be remembered, having occupied Dalmatia and Ragusa, the English and Russians fortified Lyssa, whence the English fleet stopped all the trade down that coast, caught especially the Ragusan " Argosies,"—for the town was then a flourishing little commonwealth,—and declared them prizes of war. In the meanwhile the Montenegrins, aided by a body of Russian troops, made an attempt on Ragusa, and, failing of that, burnt all the houses around the city, as one sees even now, destroying everything up to the very gates. This happened in 1809. The poor Ragusans, for no fault of their own, beyond falling into the hands of the all-powerful French, perched in their rocky nest, saw at one *coup d'œil* their villas smoking, their gardens devastated, and jolly British tars towing away their merchantmen, no doubt to the tune of "Rule Britannia," and in the best humour possible. The place has never recovered this final blow.

Ragusa has been at one time or another strongly fortified, and its fortifications remain intact, not without reason, perhaps, in the immediate vicinity of Turkish Herzegowina and Russian Montenegro. Crossing the draw-bridge along a winding road, between massive walls, one comes into a neat Italian city, "*petite*," but all in right proportions. A handsome stone fountain decorates the entrance; beyond, a wide street runs down the centre, between houses of white stone, just two stories high. The transverse streets are short, being stopped by the rocks in either direction, as though the main street had once formed a sort of gully between them, which agrees with what is related by the native historians, viz., that an arm of the sea formerly occupied this part of Ragusa. That this main street was once wider, and the houses loftier, is seen by taking notice of the house of Gundulíc, or Gondola, the patrician poet, which, before the great earthquake, was in the main row, and of the average height. Now it stands in a back street, overlooking all the rest, left as if to show posterity what had been. And the population was not to say proportionably greater; it was far more than that. At the climax of their prosperity, about the commencement of our Henry VIII.'s reign, one authority reckons them, including the suburbs, at *forty* thousand. They are now barely four or five.

It was Sunday, and in many of the churches mass going on. The men wore the national costume (with some exceptions), which looked picturesque, and almost oriental with their blue jerkins, bag breeches, scarlet caps, and bright daggers in red belts. Both sexes had on the bright scarlet slippers, or " paputze," with their sharp-pointed toes turned upwards. In other respects the dress of the women was not striking. Either they had adopted the ordinary French costume, or at least wore nothing to attract one's eye in Dalmatia. The ladies of the upper classes are rarely seen abroad. They go to mass in sedan chairs, and occupy retired spots in church, apart from public observation,—so, at least, Appendini assures us.

At the opposite end of the central street to that by which I entered from Gravosa, in a handsome little piazza, paved, like the rest of the town, after the fashion of Florence or Pisa,

stands the palace of the Rectors, by which title
the chief officer of the republic, elected
monthly by the great council of all of the
patrician order, was styled. It is a large,
square house, loftier and bigger than the
rest, but not otherwise distinguishable, dating,
however, from times anterior to the earthquake, when only the roof and upper story
fell. In this the rector used to reside with
his family, never going abroad except on
public occasions. His rank, says Appendini,
was that of prince or duke, but his power
in the state limited, being subordinate to the
legislative body, and under the surveillance of
the senate and minor council. He was treated,
however, with the dignity due to his position in the republic—was a Knight of the
Golden Spur, an honour conferred by Matthias
Corvinus, king of Hungary—had an *ex-officio*
vote in the three principal councils of state;
was robed in a silk toga, the colour of which
varied according to the seasons, together with
a black stole, the emblem of supreme com-

mand; and when he came forth from his palace was attended by his council and officers of state, and preceded by the band and the servants of the palace in red uniform.

A little further stands the cathedral, a handsome, white, Italian church, built after 1667, on the site of the former duomo, which fell with the rest at that fatal epoch. The old church is said to have owed its origin to Richard Cœur de Lion, who, being overtaken by a storm, as he was returning from the Holy Land, on the Adriatic, made a vow that he would build a church wherever he should come safely to shore. He landed eventually on the little island of La Croma, close to the Ragusan metropolis, and after his return to England sent a considerable sum of money in pursuance of his vow. By means of a dispensation from Rome, and King Richard's own consent, the originally destined site of the church was changed to that spot in the city where the cathedral has ever since stood, the Senate undertaking to build another upon the island on a scale more suitable to its size. Thus a magnificent church arose in Ragusa, which was long the finest ecclesiastical edifice in all Dalmatia.

There are a few objects of interest within the modern building, *e.g.* an Assumption, of the school of Titian; Raphael's Madonna della Seggiola, said to be authentic; a black Byzantine Madonna; the altar of the family of the illustrious Giorgi, raised to the patrician order after the earthquake, and a fine marble image of St. John Nepomuk, which the canon who took me round the cathedral said was originally intended for England. It was executed at Venice, about a century or so back, and thence shipped for its destination, but, encountering shipwreck in the Gulf, came into the hands of the Ragusans. Further particulars he could not give. Through the bishop I was enabled to see the relics, which both for splendour and intrinsic value yield, it is said, to nothing out of Rome. During the republic they might not be opened except in the presence of two senators. The origin of this sacred wealth is interesting, and connected with the history of these countries. Several were the gifts of Paulimirus, a very early Slave prince, their special benefactor, who stopped here on his return from exile in Rome; others of Margaret, queen of Dalmatia and Bosnia; but the greatest number were purchased for the Ragusans, after the Ottoman conquest, by their agents who traded throughout Roumelia and the other Turco-Slave provinces. During the French occupation under Napoleon, the treasures of the duomo were spared, apparently in consideration of the voluntary surrender the Ragusans had made of themselves. Amongst interesting specimens of ancient and modern art is the case containing the relics of St. Blaise, to whom the cathedral is dedicated, of gold, beautifully and curiously ornamented with Byzantine enamel of the eleventh and twelfth centuries; also the entire skeleton of St. Silvanus, which, being found recently with

H

the martyr's ampulla of ancient glass, containing his blood, in the catacombs, was presented by the present Pope, Pius IX., to the town of Ragusa, accompanied with a wax figure of the saint, the beauty of which will be understood by those who know the perfection to which Italian wax-work has been brought. Amongst many other precious relics is a finger of St. John Baptist, the possession of which was once made a "casus belli" between the republics of Ragusa and Venice; and some extraordinarily large pearls; also, a Bacino and Brocca, of silver, curiously wrought to imitate all sorts of aquatic reptiles, and intended, though for some reason never sent, as a present to Sigismund, king of Hungary. And, finally, what as an object of devotion surpasses all the rest, the "Pannicello," or, "our Lord's swaddling-cloth," made of "palma pesta," on which our Saviour is believed to have been first laid after His nativity in the manger.

The abundance of the precious metals at

Ragusa, from the earliest times, is wont to be accounted for by their monopoly of the trade with Bosnia, whose mountains possessed silver-mines, and the sands of whose rivers yielded a supply of gold-dust. Whether ingots were ever met with there, as at present in California and Australia, is not known; it is certain, on the other hand, that a portion of the gold came into the Ragusan market mixed with silver. The whole disappeared with the Turkish invasion and the overthrow of the Slave dynasties. The only memorials of it which remain are the bright coins, &c., which are still seen glittering in the hair of the Slave women on the Austrian frontier. It was thus the young women once carried their whole marriage portions, until they found it exposed them additionally to the scimitars and lust of the Turkish freebooters.

The bishop told me he had two outlying districts, one an ancient diocese in Herzegowina, the other at Bari, across the Adriatic, in Italy. During the ninth century the Saracens from Africa invaded this coast, and, having taken Budua, Rissano, and Cattaro, formed the siege of Ragusa, which was raised, after fifteen months' continuance, by a Greek fleet. The Saracens next fell upon Lombardy, and then, after a while, seized upon Bari. The Greeks, the Slave princes, and the Ragusans, in alliance with the Pope and the king of France, pursued them, and, overthrowing them in a great battle on Mount Gargano, retook the town, which remaining some while in the hands of the republic, the spiritual supervision of its see was permanently annexed to Ragusa.

Outside the gates on the southern side is the Bazaar, or *Caravanna dei Turchi*, who come three times a-week to sell cattle and buy clothes in exchange. It is an open space with pens and booths, like a suburban Smithfield on a smaller scale. Formerly the Turks were forbidden, on pain of death, to enter the town. Their own frontier is a few miles off, across the mountains.

Since the calamitous event of the seventeenth century, although there has been as yet no recurrence of such a catastrophe, minor shocks are felt continually; nay, one occurred about ten days before I was there. Forasmuch, then, as more than one disastrous earthquake is recorded in ages gone by, one cannot but wonder that, in spite of such warnings, the inhabitants have still clung to the site of their middle-age city, instead of returning to the more ancient Epidaurus, or migrating to the immediate vicinity of Gravosa. In either situation, but especially the latter, they would have had a far better harbour, where, indeed, even as things are, *i.e.*, with all its present disadvantages of distance from the city, Lloyd's steamer prefers to anchor, while the experience of all ages since the dawn of history declares the safety of its shores as regards that fatal danger, from which the actual site of the city will be never free. May not the present fallen state of this once prosperous community be the consequence of this strange unwillingness or incapacity to take advantage of such plain suggestions of common sense?

The town is neat and clean, strongly reminding one of Venice, and evidently the offspring of the same age and chain of ideas. The spot on which it stands has at least the merit of great picturesque beauty. A multitude of olives planted around give it their peculiar verdure, and the outlying villas, many of which have been restored, a look of cheerfulness. The roads are excellent near the town, and I was assured there were beautiful views within the reach of enterprising pedestrians.

Under the republic Ragusa was an archbishopric; and Englishmen will be interested by the recollection that an ex-archbishop, Bernardo, in the reign of King John was collated to the see of Carlisle, and thus happened to be present at the funeral of St. Hugh, bishop of Lincoln, A.D. 1200.*

* See Roger of Wendover's Chronicle, ad annum.

V.

THE BOCCHE—CATTARO AND OAFS—BUDUA AND THE
TURKISH FRONTIER.

THE sudden cessation of that uncomfortable,
up-and-down mode of progression which
steamers are wont to assume under the
influence of a gale from the south-west in
"Adria," and the nearly simultaneous freshening of the temperature, brought us all upon
deck. We were steaming rapidly along a
wide channel of dark, deep, still water, sometimes broader, sometimes narrower, and ever
and anon running up into long, winding
creeks, between lofty, barren hills; while
right ahead towered the black and seemingly
inaccessible heights of Montenegro, bleak and
bare, above our heads. The steep mountain
sides relaxed a little close to the margin of
the sea, where a narrow rim of cultivation,

studded with numerous *paesetti*, or hamlets,
ornamented the water's edge: here a white
church just covered the surface of a rock
standing up above the blue waves; and there
a priest's house on another hard-by seemed,
as our gliding course gave them both an
apparent motion, like Delos of old, to follow
and minister to it.   Around gambolled innumerable dolphins, flinging themselves far out
of the water, whether in pursuit of prey, or
from pure joyousness, I know not; but
thereby affording better amusement for the
present than omen of weather for the morrow,
as Pliny's " Prognostics " inform us.

Towards the bottom of the Bocca it grew
dark and gloomy.   At length, on a small
promontory projecting from a rugged and
almost perpendicular precipice between two
streams (Fuimara and Sgorgo), which rush
out of the rock behind, appeared the town
of Cattaro, called by the natives " Kotar:"
a situation fortified and inaccessible by
nature, and hence, according to local tra-

dition, chosen for their final resting-place by the remains of the Avares after that, having overrun the Roman province, and taken Salonæ, they were forced to retreat before the overwhelming force of the Croats. A castle, in a strong position according to the notions of former times, rises on the first rocky height above, around which winds the long, zig-zag path leading to the frontier of the Montenegrins. This town is another miniature Venice, containing a few thousand inhabitants, with pavé, piazze, and everything just on the same pattern.

We here took leave of our steamer, which was to return on the morrow to Zara, and I hastened to go into Cattaro and secure a room somewhere, knowing by past experience that one does not always get such accommo- dation as one could wish in these old towns. I was fortunate on this occasion to get a bedroom, not indeed at an inn, for of inns there is not one in all Cattaro; nor in a private lodging, for every lodging is occupied by the numerous Government employés, but at a Trattoria.* On my return even this was engaged; and the master was proposing to remove the cloth from one of his dining tables for my couch, when I luckily received a kind invitation from a friend I had made on my first visit.

To proceed: the character of the place is not badly represented in its cathedral, a Byzantine building of the eighth century, with two towers, massively built, and sombre inside, the only colours being black and white. with heavy, dark oak furniture, and three altars at the end of a corresponding number of aisles. Six solid stone columns, with composite capitals, support the short nave and choir. They are supposed to have been transported thither from the temple of Jupiter at Rhizonium, not far distant, on the shores of the Bocche, being the town whither Queen Teuta fled after her defeat. Round Roman arches spring from the capitals,

* That is, in English, a cook's shop.

agreeing in character with the rest of the building.

Everything looks as sombre as if it were intended to harmonize with those deep shadows which the surrounding mountains throw around. The men wear dark-coloured brown or chocolate breeches and mantles, which, if white, are yet edged with black. Their cap is red, in this alone distinguished from the Montenegrins, who frequent Cattaro in large numbers, especially on market-days, and mix no livelier hue with the black and (would-be) white colours of their costume. If the Cattarans be descended from the Avares, a race akin to Turks and Magyars, they have forgotten their original tongue, only the usual languages of this coast being understood here, viz., German, Italian, and their own dialect of Slave. They were long under Venetian rule, but are now Austrian subjects. In religion, too, an alteration has come over them; for they were nearly all, up to the beginning of this century, Catholics; but during the last fifty years, two-thirds have become "Disunited Greeks." This latter change has arisen in great measure from the emigration of the old inhabitants and the immigration of families from the mountain. In short, it would appear that the place is growing more and more Montenegrine.

The fact is, that the towns on all this coast have changed. Partly, the stream of commerce has left them since the discovery of the Cape of Good Hope, and flows through other channels; partly, the tastes and requirements of European society are altered, and people seek out new abodes.

"Tempora mutantur, et nos mutamur."

During the rough and warlike ages which succeeded the irruption of the northern nations into the more civilized provinces of the Roman empire, the first object which men sought after was security from external violence. Having provided to the best of their means for this, they brought their habits of life, their business, their wants, their recreations, into unison with the circumstances in which they

ALBANIA, AND MONTENEGRO. **117**

found themselves. The limited commerce of those days was forced to follow, not so much the most convenient as the only practicable paths, and to direct itself to those ports, however otherwise unsuitable, where merchants could meet and transact their affairs without fear, and bestow their goods under the protection of laws and a police whose domain extended little, if at all, beyond city walls. Correlative to this state of things were the scientific attainments and mechanical powers of the age. Limited in their actual extent, a bar was likewise set to their further development. Until the rise of experimental philosophy in the seventeenth century, authority held unbounded sway, and scientific discovery was a term unknown. There could be no progress, and the treatises of the ancients were, notwithstanding a few great incidental inventions, simply stereotyped. Hence, what *did* for one age continued to *do* for another; or, if any alteration were required, it was in obedience to the small views of a local and practical experience, as when the Ragusans left the site of the classic Epidaurus for that of their present city, certainly not from any enlarged and scientific views of the requirements of civilised life or the probable future channels of commerce.

Thus it has come to pass, that places which were for ages emporia of commerce, like old institutions whose serviceableness is gone by, lose their *prestige*, suffer a general decay, and finally either change their character, or are utterly swept away by the first storm of war or revolution which passes over them. Of such changes this coast exhibits many remarkable instances, amongst which Venice, Ragusa, and Cattaro are specimens, widely differing in scale, but not the less examples of and witnesses to the same phenomenon. Cattaro lies under special disabilities peculiar to itself: it is placed at the very extremity of the Bocche, four hours' row from Castel Nuovo, where the narrow embouchure opens into the Adriatic. It is overshadowed by the gloomy heights of

Montenegro, which cut off the sun's rays in winter, whilst their reflection against the mountains' sides causes a dull, oppressive heat, rendering the town an unwholesome residence in summer. Moreover, until quite lately, it was exposed to the depredations of the Montenegrins, who, during the anarchical years of 1848-9, committed serious ravages round about. More recently, the well-timed intervention of Austria having saved them from the arms of Omer Pasha, they have felt themselves under an obligation to that power, which the Emperor Francis Joseph is careful to keep alive by presents and good offices. Were it otherwise, possessing, since the war, some half-dozen cannon, they might readily bombard Cattaro from the neighbouring heights, and, having a numerous party of immigrant fellow-countrymen amongst the inhabitants, become formidable at any moment to the Austrian supremacy within its walls.

The fatigue of an early walk at Ragusa, followed by a rough passage as far as the

Bocche, and then all the turmoil of getting ashore at Cattaro, rendered one indisposed for paying visits and making new acquaintances; so I deferred my letters of introduction until a more favourable opportunity, and wandered out round the head of the bay, to enjoy the last half-hour of daylight. Crossing the bridge, which spans one of the rivers shortly after it has sprung tumultuously from the base of the rock, and entered on its straight and impetuous career to the sea, I followed the road along the shore. Numerous parties of soldiers, belonging to the Austrian garrison, which is large, and officers and ladies, were returning from the *cafés* or cabarets, or "tea-gardens," as they would be in England, where all ranks had been amusing themselves. "Publics" and "*cafés*," *in*-doors and "out," are quite essential to Austria. In no part of the empire does one miss them, and no one surely has had greater influence on social life there, than that Turkish spy—a Pole by birth— to whom the first *café* in Vienna, towards the end of the seventeenth century, owes its origin.

The use of coffee and cafés in Turkey is mentioned by Lord Bacon at the beginning of the same century, but in a way to show that both were then regarded as exotics in Europe. " They have in Turkey," says he, " a drink called·coffee, made of a berry of the same name, as black as soot,"—he meant, of course, *after* roasting,—" and of a strong scent, but not aromatical, which they take beaten into powder, in water, as hot as they can drink it: and they take it, and sit at it in their coffeehouses, which are like our taverns." "This drink," he adds, "comforteth the brain and heart, and helpeth *digestion*" *—a matter considered of no minor importance in Austria, and which has doubtless had its full share in contributing to the universal prevalence of the place deriving its name therefrom. Cafés, however, have attained to a far more extended use than the

* "Sylva sylvarum."

J

mere decoction and discussion of that beverage. Accordingly Austrians breakfast at their café, read their paper there, there play at billiards, there take their coffee after dinner, and their ice a little later, and last, but not least, there smoke their pipes while they play at cards and talk of everything except religion and politics. In short, all but dining and sleeping, they live there, and especially the military, whose ordinary day life seems to be composed of three constituents, "dinner, drill, and café."

I had proposed to myself a walk round the head of the bay, to get a view of the Black Mountain from the opposite side; but, finding the evening coming on, all parties' faces turned towards Cattaro, and nothing very interesting in the gloomy rock, which was additionally blackened by the harbingers of night, and rain gathering over head, I turned townwards likewise, intending to go and look for the Greeks and Lombards in order to arrange our departure for the next morning.

Of course there was but one rendezvous; so, retracing my steps by the little cabarets, I adjourned to the principal café in the Piazza-del-duomo, where I soon found my Lombard companions already provided with coffee, pipes, and newspapers, if the latter, which had been on our cabin table on board the steamer for a week, could merit that name. They had already agreed with the Greeks, who had gone to pass the evening with some of their congeners, not to go without us on the morrow. There were besides ourselves several parties of officers in the room playing at whist, and we had not been long arrived when the physician in chief of the district came in and entered into our little coterie. He was a well-informed person, as a doctor should be; was acquainted with Sir G. Wilkinson, when he was here collecting materials for his book on Dalmatia and Montenegro, and told me he had himself written on the Morlachs in a Milanese medical journal a few years ago, that is to say, more especially on

their diseases and habits of life. His opinion
was that they are a race of Slaves, although
their particular derivation was unknown.

All this, however interesting to me, was
not particularly so to the Lombards, who,
caring not for the Morlachs, nor, as Italians,
partaking of the Austrian apathy on the subject of politics, much preferred to discuss
the prevailing question of the day, which was,
of course, the impending war, and, to my
surprise—not knowing as yet the suspicion
to which Englishmen, and indeed all foreigners
travelling on this coast, are considered open—
they directed their conversation to *me*, as if
I must know something more about what was
likely to happen than other people. At the
time I could not imagine what led them to
make so remarkable a blunder : but no doubt,
in common with some other sapient people
I afterwards fell in with, they thought they
had a reason, though I have never been able
to make out that it was anything more conclusive than the fact that I travelled with a

note-book and a thermometer! Be this as it may, instead of inquiring my opinion of the weather, and ascertaining if I were or were not of those to whom

> ".... nunquam imprudentibus imber
> Obfuit ....."

they set me down as a novel species of "political weathercock," and to be interrogated as such. Nor was this, if the beginning, the end of it; for before I had finished my travels, my fame, which, as they say, ever "crescit eundo," had magnified me into a regular "scarecrow" at last, converted my annotations atmospheric into calculations strategic, until by some strange process of reasoning the authorities themselves were fairly brought to the conclusion that I must be employed by— at this time their great bugbear throughout Austria—my Lord Palmerston himself!

The next morning, October 17th, it was, alas! pouring with wet, as *we, travellers,* believed the ordinary state of things at Cattaro! Here was an end to all hopes of climbing the hill to-day to Cetinja. To let

alone that the road is up the side of a very
nearly perpendicular precipice, the mountain
was quite enveloped in such dense clouds
that no one up there could have seen a foot
before his nose.   So I went and called on my
acquaintance of last night, the doctor, at the
"*circolo*," that is, the house in which the
local government is conducted, to ask his
opinion, not medically, but first atmospheri-
cally, and secondly politically, as to the present
feasibility of making a short detour into the
neighbouring Turkish province of Albania,
which is of course part of Turkey.   He did
not seem to know much about the latter;
about the former he shook his head, looked
very blank, and said it sometimes rained here
for three weeks in that way without intermis-
sion.   On which alone—not to mention my
own opinion—I immediately conceived great
hopes of getting on that evening, being too
well up to the tricks of doctors to be much
afraid of portentous looks, especially considering that we were at *Cattaro*, that he was
an agreeable companion, and that, though

strangers, we had *some things in common* in
our pursuits. So, shortly wishing him " good
morning," and promising to come and see
him again *"without fail, if the rain did not
stop,"* I went on to another recommendation,
" Monsignore il Vicario Capitolare," whom
I found most kind and hospitable. He was
a man of letters, had been formerly a professor at Spalato, and, as a Dalmatian, was of
course interested in Slave literature. He was
just proposing to me to come and see some
antiquities, and especially the Reliquary of
the Cathedral, which is celebrated, when, lo!
out came the sun. " Aha ! " thought I, as the
worthy doctor came to mind, then begging
permission to continue my wanderings, and
apologising for the abruptness of my departure,—since, perhaps, bad weather would return ere long, to which the good Vicario quite
assented,—I was presently trotting along the
same road as last night, mounted on a villan-
ous hack and preceded by a Cattaran, clad in
the usual costume of the Bocca, armed to the

teeth with gun, pistols, and dagger, and stalking away before me like one of the Highlanders in "Rob Roy" or "Waverley."

We crossed the "Sgorgo" by the formerly mentioned bridge, wound up the hill behind it, getting a magnificent view of Cattaro and the "Tserna Gora," or Black Mountain, from the fort at the top; thence continued over the undulating hills overgrown with myrtle in beautiful flower, and arbutus in scarcely less beautiful fruit; then down through a plain sown with maize between hedges, in which ripe pomegranates hung in wild profusion amidst the common "traveller's joy." We left a Greek convent on our left, again ascended the hogsback of a promontory running out into the sea, once more descended and found ourselves just as evening came on close to a little gulf upon the sands of which stands the small but strongly fortified town of Budua: for, as will be long ere this understood, instead of attempting the dizzy zigzag up to Cetinja, I had deserted my steamer companions, both

Lombards and Greeks, and was trying to find an easier, though far longer and more circuitous, route to the top of the Tserna Gora than by all accounts, confirmed by distant ocular observations, is the direct road from Cattaro.

After threading our way through the narrow, little, dark streets of Budua in the dusk, we pulled up at last at what my guide termed " the Inn," and the people of the place dignified by the title of the "Veneziano," inside which was a large drinking chamber on the ground floor, or, to speak more accurately, to which the ground was the only floor, with a ladder staircase leading up into a very uninviting, dirty bedroom, furnished with a bed of about the same dimensions, as near as I could judge, as that of which the town of Ware is said to be justly proud, and which was, they add, the mode six hundred years ago ! As they had nothing to eat in the house, and did not seem at all sanguine about procuring anything, I went out to forage in the unlit streets for myself, and also to try to find the " Canonico

Derrocco, paroco," *i.e.*, "Curé," of Budua, to
whom I was recommended. By dint of perseverance I bought some bread and cheese in
a shop, found a cup of "caffé nero" in its
proper habitat, and finally sought the "paroco"
in his, hard-by. He was, however, not at
home. Where should I look for him? In the
café, of course: and there he was all the while
at a table in a corner playing a rubber at
whist with the municipal authorities and the
officer in command, a nephew of General
Wimpfen at Trieste. He soon rose and came
up to me—a remarkable looking person, rather
below the middle stature, with nearly black
hair, dark, piercing, brilliant eyes, and a good-
natured but very intelligent expression of
countenance: in a word, quite the physiog-
nomy of the place of his nativity, viz. Ragusa.
His information was useful as well as interesting, and after a short conversation, in the
course of which he told me that Budua was
half Catholic and half Greek, and that there
had been little distress here compared with

what we had had from the failure of crops, both grain and grapes, in the north of the Gulf this year, I took leave and retired to my monster bed.

In the morning I was soon ready, and but too happy to leave such wretched accommodation:—perhaps there was a clean strip in the bed, if one had but known whereabouts to find it, but it was, I suppose, too much to expect people to wash such big sheets, except at solemn stated intervals. As to their coffee, it was an abominable *farrago*. So, bestriding my Rosinante, I proceeded along the beach, enjoying the lovely day and dashing waves, which almost surrounded us as they encroached around the bright green rocks, which seemed as if they had been cleft during a convulsion of nature from some great mountain of *verde antique*. And Budua has been subject to earthquakes. It was, for instance, entirely overthrown by that which ruined Ragusa nearly two hundred years ago. Soon came the village of Castel Lastua in sight,

being the last habitations in the Austrian
dominions on this side. Here I must leave
my horse, and find instead a mule recommended by the *canonico*, and conducted by a
Greek, or rather Slave of the Greek faith.

Castel Lastua is a village in the middle of a
bend of the sea, containing barely half a
dozen houses, and some Austrian barracks.
However, as I had eaten but little since noon
of the day before, and had had some hard
work meanwhile, I fondly hoped to get some
eatable dinner in the little cabaret. But
vain was the thought! Dinner, indeed, I
got: but eatable!—that was quite another
matter. They had nothing but the black,
half-straw bread—coarse as that which the
Flemings give their horses—called *pan mili-*
tare, and some lumps of bullock's liver, as
hard as iron, which reminded one unpleasantly
of " Count Fathom's " repast in the robbers'
den of the Black Forest, when they served
him up his chopped bridle, preparatory to the
pie garnished with men's, instead of pigeons'

claws! But let no one be afraid; the second course did not appear, and if the meat were once a bridle or saddle, for it was hard enough for either, at least it was not *mine*. A young Austrian soldier came in to eat,— that is, to *try* to eat, at the same table with me, who, though but a private, was evidently of a superior class by his features, and found the liver much as I did. Perhaps he was a victim of the conscription only; more probably, he was forced to serve in the ranks for a political offence : at any rate, he seemed very discontented with his present lot in general, and the liver in particular. He was anxious to learn of me if I thought the war which was impending would become general, and Austria, as many expected, break with Turkey and her allies. Such an event would have been regarded as no small boon by the discontented Austrian soldiers, as they could then have deserted across the frontier without fear of being sent back. He spoke German, which no one there was likely to understand,

and was thus able to express his wishes without fear of discovery.

The mule was, no doubt, an excellent beast, and very fast in her paces,—as I had been assured by the *canonico*, who directed me where to find her—but she evinced an obstinate determination to send me flying over her ears from the moment I took my seat upon her back, and for a good while afterwards, by flinging out in every direction : a trick which I have noticed to be not uncommon with mules at starting, they seeming to think this a pleasant and facetious mode of cutting short so burthensome a business as a day's march. *Her* master, however, and *my* guide, *Marco Jovof Perasich*, as he called himself, who was, besides, nothing less than *Capo di Villa*, and, as he also told me, an *uomo di famiglia,*—which meant, practically, that if we were, by chance, robbed and murdered while in company, *my* executors might come upon *his* for certain pecuniary redress, —exhorted me to stick fast ; which, indeed,

I was fain to do, without his exhortations, and with all my might, not seeing any fun in being cast violently upon the large stones of which the road was made, which were none of the smoothest; nor thinking even his pecuniary liability much satisfaction to rely on, so far as I was concerned; even supposing it to extend to such a case, which seems rather a nice point. After a time, however, the mule, giving over her attempts on the integrity of my seat, went more pleasantly, and being, as I observed, a fast beast, we quickly cleared the actual frontier, which a lofty pole was erected to mark. A corporal's guard of Austrian soldiers lay on the grass just beyond, beneath the shade of a great tree, awaiting the coming of a deserter, who was expected to be sent back from Osman Pasha of Scutari.

Forthwith a wild and most romantic scene opened itself. Everything like a road ceased. We followed little bye-paths, the dry bed of a torrent, or a sheep-walk, or, at best, the narrow footway of the peasants. Above us, to our left, rose the richly-coloured, red mountains of Albania; while, to our right, lofty rocks, not wanting in verdure, shut out the view of the sea. On one of these cliffs were the ruins of an old town, with two fortresses, which, in the days of its strength, bore the boasting name of *Nechaj*, signifying in Illyrian, "without care," in allusion to its supposed impregnability; and a little further, overlooking the sea, the dismantled convent of Rotatz, a celebrated Greek monastery, where some of the oldest monuments of the Slave language extant were long preserved. In the fifteenth century, however, it was occupied as a military position by the Venetians against the Turks, and finally blown up and abandoned. On we went, through thickets and uncultivated fields, with just here and there a patch of dug ground near some lonely cottage, built of rough stones; or a few olives or figs, and a little plot of *grano Turco*,* near the path. Yet the hedges abounded in

* Indian corn.

pomegranates, and the natural vegetation was
so rich,—so rank, one might say,—that the
reflection often forced itself: "What might
not here be done by a little cultivation!"

Soon we cross a bridge in one of the better
paths; a Turkish inscription in Arabic letters
relates that the founder has made it for the
good of humanity and the benefit of his soul.
A few peasantry are scattered about working
at their little plots, and here a woman
washes clothes by the side of a running
stream. Her dress is *little* different from
what I have already described in Dalmatia,
but her look, *much*. "Mai danno gli occhj,"
said my guide to me, after asking her the
road; to which she replied with eyes fixed
steadfastly on the ground, and withal a sort of
proud, sullen air too. Next we meet a party
of Turks, in single file, as the narrowness of
the road compels. The escort denotes persons
of rank. The Signori are on horseback,
strongly armed with pistols and *hangjar*.
Three or four men on foot, their long guns

K

slung on their backs, follow. They are con-
ducting the unfortunate deserter in the Turkish dress of his adoption to his doom! We
reach the sea-shore; a melancholy Han or
Khan stands just out of reach of the waves;
and now, one hour more, and we shall be at
Antivari, which lies a few miles inland, or at
another Khan farther on, but also by the sea-
side; which latter my guide vehemently
recommends, declaring that we can hardly go
to Antivari to-night, the roads are so bad,
&c.; and that at the next Khan—*el Han*, he
called it—I should find "L'Agenzia di Lloyd,
e tutto quanto" (Lloyd's agency, and all I
can want for the night). So, unmindful of the
adage, "Never trust a Greek," I yield, and,
for my folly, on arrival, am not a little dis-
gusted to find only Lloyd's *warehouse*, in a
perfectly lonely spot, and the necessity of
passing the night supperless, as well as din-
nerless, on a big box, or bale of merchandise,
in the same room with four rude men,
including the guide, who, on my complaining

of the deception, were anything but agreeable
or polite.

Notwithstanding, I slept soundly, though
my box, for a bed, was something hardish,
until I was awoke about midnight, by a
tremendous hurricane, rain pouring in torrents,
wind, thunder, and lightning, striving, as it
seemed, for the mastery. It was really an
awful night; and, except the Khan had been
a new one, and built under the eye of Lloyd's
agent, I should have feared its being swept
away. The ' *Capo di Villa* ' and his friends
snored through it all—but, during the pauses
of the storm, I heard Allahs! and Mashallahs!
Wallas! and Billas! proceeding from a
neighbouring apartment, wherein an elderly
Mussulman was reposing—for, in these Hans,
the Mussulmans and Christians are provided
with distinct rooms, when their size will
permit. At length the hurricane ceased,
and, when daylight broke, and we got on
our legs again, all was still enough, except
the droppings of the rain from the eaves,

and the roar of distant streams swollen into floods.

As soon as the deluge allowed us to move, about eight A.M., I again mounted, and this time, a little bay Turkish horse,—which, from its goodness, was probably one of those left six or seven months previously, by Omar Pasha's expedition, when he withdrew from the invasion of Montenegro,—and, after floundering through a sea of mud and water, often up to the girths in the meadows, which were flooded far and near, eventually got upon the hill close beside, but opposite to the ancient and once Italian city of Antivari. On the ascent, somewhat above the level of the town, stand two rough cottages, built *à la Suisse*, with deep, projecting roofs, and open wooden staircases outside, to reach the first floor, on which, as in all Southern Europe, the family reside. The first is the abode of the Austrian Consul and his wife—both from Ragusa. The second, of Monsignor Poaten, a Franciscan monk, and Catholic bishop of this diocese. The latter was from home; by the former I was hospitably entertained for a day and a night, while I rested from the fatigues of the last two days. Hard by was the little church or chapel, a most unpretending, barn-like room, built of bricks, and tiled over. The Turkish authorities, it appears, allow of no external symbol or ornament whatsoever. Leave to build a church at all for Christian worship, until quite lately, was most difficult to obtain.

VI.

As soon as I had rested a little from the
fatigues of the last two days, which had been
considerable, I went to call at the Bishop's,
hard by. He was from home, but I found
his chaplain, who kindly undertook, in the
absence of the Vice-Consul (called to the sea-
coast by the arrival of an Austrian steamer),
to accompany me to the residence of the Bey
of the district, who lived at a short distance
outside the town, to pay my respects to him
as the governor, and request permission to see
the interior of the old town.

Accordingly we set out, following the road
I had traversed on my first arrival, through
the Bazaar and the Turkish burial-ground,

which extended for some space on either side, covered with little rounded pillars (the tops of some carved into a rude imitation of a turban, and inscribed with sentences in Arabic from the Koran), here and there interspersed with little mausoleums, or stone canopies supported on four pillars. Thence we turned down to the river, and finally reached the Bey's abode across a bridge of planks of very rude construction. The house stood close upon the river side, having an open gallery covered with a verandah on the first floor, to which a staircase on the outside conducted. Here 'Selim' Bey himself. with his eldest son, a lad of twelve or fourteen, was sitting in a small divan, surrounded with sofas, and shrouded from the public gaze by curtains. He was a fat, red-looking man, rather above the middle height, with a good-natured, but thoroughly uneducated expression of face, and the manner of one who, though not unamiable, would be apt to be provoked, if thwarted; in short, the sort of person who might do you a kindness, provided you did not get into his path, but would play the *rôle* of a strong and fiery bull if you did. He was seated crosslegged in the ordinary Turkish costume of loose breeches, with white stockings, and slipperless feet. He received me very graciously, as an Englishman; called for pipes and coffee, said a few words in Illyrian, and then continued the conversation in Turkish, which was translated for my benefit by his dragoman into Italian, which, though the language of the coast, the Bey did not appear to understand one word of. Of course, the war and the state of Europe were matters of chief interest to him.

On my request to see the inside of the town, he at once replied in the negative, touching his head, to imply that, without leave from the Pasha of Scutari, it would be as much as his life was worth to admit a foreigner in the present crisis, for he added, significantly, "*We* also are servants."

I shortly took my leave, not displeased with him; for indeed his manners to me were

the reverse of discourteous. But the Vice-
consul's wife afterwards confirmed my first
impression. He had, she said, lately divorced
his wife, the mother of the son I saw with him,
for no fault whatsoever, real or pretended,
and, on her interceding with him for the
unhappy lady, he replied, "To please you,
Madam, I will marry another as soon as you
like; but nothing shall ever induce me to
receive back the one I have divorced." The
chaplain also, who had been some years on
the mission, drew an awful picture of the
immorality of the Turks; for, if such be their
treatment of women who are of families on
equality with themselves, it may be imagined
how they would use their inferiors. The
Albanian Mahometan, it is to be observed,
does not marry more than one wife at a time,
being too poor to keep a seraglio, which this
would entail; but he makes up for it, so to
speak, by divorces and concubinage with his
female servants, and poorer neighbours of the
weaker sex—and they, too, generally Chris-

tians—whose children are commonly destroyed before or after birth, and then buried secretly for fear of the *vendetta*—the revenge of her relations, which the shedding of blood, when known, solemnly imposes upon them.

Hence in the marriage contract the share of the dower to be returned in case of divorce is always specified, so that when personal beauty passes, no bond of union remains. " The women have no pursuits in common with their husbands, and are quite without education. Even the Turkish gentlemen of rank can often scarcely read or write, and a Turkish lady despises all those graceful occupations which we regard as well-nigh essential to the sex." * To this, amongst other causes, it must be attributed, that you never see women in the company of men. The sexes cannot mix in honourable pursuits, and thus the civilising effect which their

---

* The quotations are from an article on the "Christians in Albania," written by the author of these letters for a magazine, in 1854.

mutual presence would have upon each other is entirely lost.

While the state of domestic morality is thus low, the corrupt administration of public justice is even worse. " The judge is venal, —perhaps himself the offender. The rajah, or Christian subject of the sultan, is a slave, and cannot help himself; his oath is of no avail." A poor man must surrender his property, however necessary to him, on demand, to the local governor, or go to prison, a noisome place at Antivari, beneath the Bey's house, abounding in vermin and other horrors. " In fact," to quote again words already in print, " for the poor there is literally no justice; it is all bought and sold. The pashas and beys pay high prices to obtain their respective governments, receiving no pay themselves except what they get from the people, from whom, therefore, they exact the utmost they can, in the way of bribes and similar impositions in order, first, to indemnify and then to enrich themselves." It cost, for instance, one of these Beys £1,200 at Constantinople to gain, and maintain himself in his lucrative post. No wonder that justice comes to be made as far as possible a means of gain. Is a murder committed, the Bey's officers go and seize, " not the murderer, but his moveable property, which is confiscated to their master, and, making a bonfire of his house, they leave the culprit to escape into the woods, or, in short, wherever he pleases."

" In default of law and its due administration, the practice of *revenge* is not unnaturally regarded as a duty, even amongst the Christian inhabitants. The last words uttered by a dying Albanian to his son, or next-of-kin, are commonly, ' Vendicate me ; ' and the injunction is only too faithfully obeyed by the descendant, as soon as he finds an opportunity of killing any member of the family who did the injury ; and then *they* in their turn feel bound by the same savage antichristian custom. It is perhaps only what must be expected amongst a brave, energetic people, with arms in their hands, subjected for ages to a semi-barbarian rule, with no education, no schools, no churches, and no sort of effectual administration of public justice."

" All who profess themselves Christians are required to pay tribute, which, however small the nominal sum, is yet enough, with other inflictions, and in so poor a country, to tempt numbers to feign themselves Mahometans, in order to escape it." Thirty-five piastres—six shillings of our money—" is a very heavy burden to a peasantry who have literally no money, and no means of procuring any. . . . Yet the poverty of the country cannot be justly attributed to want of industry in the Christian population; certainly not to the want of an enterprising spirit, for many of them go as far as Constantinople in search of service."

Although the town within the walls of Antivari was thus sealed to my personal inspection, I learnt from those I was with that the old Venetian fortifications stood untouched just as they were three or four hundred years ago; that the streets and churches (only the latter turned into mosques) remained without further alteration, and that even the very names of the families who reside there are many of them Venetian, their unhappy ancestors having become renegades at the time of the Turkish conquest, to escape expulsion, or perhaps death. "The Turks never repair anything," and it is said that if the authorities are asked why, they answer, "To what purpose? We are strangers; we come from afar, and are here to-day; but who knows if we shall be here to-morrow?"

The following morning I started at seven with fresh horse and guide, this time an Albanian Catholic, for Scutari. The road we took ran first beneath the town, across the river, and then turned up the hill, on part of which Antivari is built, keeping along an elevated causeway of large, rough stones fitted together, which sometimes showed in its construction superior skill and workmanship, sometimes so badly repaired, that it was difficult for the horse which carried me to pass; especially since over the steeper acclivities it led in the form of flights of rough, irregular steps, leaving it evident that the engineer who planned it did not contemplate the use of wheeled carriages. This continued nearly the whole way to Scutari, except where it was interrupted by the infamous state of its repair, a grievance to the traveller of no recent date, for its course was obliterated in one part for a long way by old thorn-trees, which could only have commenced their slow growth after the beaten track had been effaced, and the wayfarer compelled to choose his path through the adjoining fields, amidst the mire of which we had to flounder for some half-mile before we could regain the stones.

Just as we started, and before we had well cleared the walls and suburbs of the town, but were quite out of sight of people,

we were joined by two Turkish women in
large dark capotes, the hoods drawn over their
faces, and slippers on their bare feet. They,
too, were going to Scutari, and wished to
take advantage of our escort. Eventually
they kept up with us the whole day, though,
judging by the whiteness of their hands and
feet, they could not have been accustomed to
such long journeyings on foot. At first they
walked behind us, closely veiled, with much
apparent shyness; but the heat of the sun,
and the severity of a protracted march along
so rough a road, soon made them less coy.
They dropped their veils, and, pulling off their
slippers, took every *natural* means, according
to the notions of the women of those countries, to help themselves along, including, by-
the-bye, giving their cloaks to my horse to
carry. Both were young and well-looking;
the youngest quite a girl, of seventeen,
perhaps; the other about ten years older.
The day was fine, and the scenery lovely,
through a fine wild champaign country,

skirted with woods, and the deep blue mountains rising above for the background. Of cultivation, except a patch of maize here and there, I could see none. A cow or two, and a few sheep, mixed with goats, fed in the rough fields, which were scattered, few and far between, along the roadside. The sheep, both black and white, and some horned, seemed to have tufts growing on their foreheads; their fleece elsewhere being long and ragged, between wool and hair, so that they looked like English, long-woolled doormats on legs. Though I saw no pomegranates on the hedges, as the day before yesterday, my "vetturino" — such was my guide's proper appellative—brought me one of first-rate size and sweetness in the beginning of our march. I suspect it was garden-grown; but this fruit is renowned in the neighbourhood of Antivari. At Scutari they abound also, but of a harsh, rough-tasted sort. About mid-day we waded through a swollen brook, and, finding a nice piece of turf on the opposite bank, sat down, in three parties, to our

respective dinners; that is to say, the Mussulman women in one place, my guide in
another, and myself in a third. In half an
hour we were again *en route*, and, as the
shades of evening drew on, about six o'clock,
P.M., reached a long wooden bridge across the
wide river, along the side of which the road
for the last hour or so had been winding.
This river is the Drino, and here, where it
runs out of the lake, is at least as wide as
the Thames below Teddington. Beyond the
bridge came the Bazaar, where I halted by
myself for ten minutes, while my Vetturino
went to escort the poor "ladies," who were
getting thoroughly knocked up, and had,
besides, never been in Scutari before, to the
Khan, where they were to pass the night. By
this time it was dark; and when, for nearly
another hour, we kept on still traversing the
same kind of pavement as before, now
between high walls, now among grave-
stones, still seeing no houses, I at length
inquired, with much *naïveté*, and to the
guide's no small amazement, *when* we should

reach Scutari, and received for answer, to my no less astonishment, that it had been Scutari ever since we left the Bazaar! Where, then, were the houses? Low-roofed, and wide-spread, they were completely concealed from our ken, as we passed along, by their garden, or, more strictly speaking, *orchard* walls, within which each was enclosed. Thus widely does Scutari differ from Antivari; the latter remains as it was when a Christian town, but the former, cramped by no city walls, and arranged after Turkish notions, has all the air of an Oriental city transplanted into Europe. In short, I seemed to be always in the suburbs. And, as no artificial light from that glory of modern civilization, *gas*, or even from the more primitive lamp or candle, assisted the *eye* to dispel its illusion, so neither, though we were actually penetrating into a city of many thousand inhabitants, and the capital of a pashalic, did the *ear* reveal its proximity.

Nothing is more striking than the quiet and orderly, nay, silent state of a Turkish town at night.   No voices of the eager buyer or the yet more ardent seller, no throng of passers-by in pursuit of business or pleasure, with their noisy footfalls; no theatres, no places of public resort, no cries, no clamour, no busy hum of men, that unfailing concomitant in all ages of our western cities.   Nay, to its praise be it said, "no haunts of ill-fame contaminate its precincts; no sounds of drunken revelry disturb its streets;" no noisy brawls alarm its peaceful citizens. "After nightfall the streets are empty; each family has retired to its own abode: and if any one appears in the public ways, it is a solitary person with a light, perhaps going to seek the doctor, or on some other errand of necessity or charity.   A solemn stillness reigns, which is broken only by the guard* going round to see that all is safe, and to

* Forcibly recalling "the watchmen that go about the city" of the Canticles.

remove, if haply they should fall in with such, any disorderly person, or even the idle wanderer, who ventures to roam abroad at such an hour without ostensible object."

The house we now entered differed nothing in plan from those I have already described at Antivari, except that it was larger, and stood in its own inclosure, as aforesaid. M. Bonatti, the Vice-Consul, received me in the usual sofa'd divan, and with much hospitality. He was a native of Corfu, and, though the representative of England in this place, spoke no English, nor yet French, but Italian only.

The next day it was necessary that I should attend the Pasha's divan, more especially if I adhered to my determination to proceed over the lake to the frontier of Montenegro: an undertaking of no little difficulty, as some thought, since hostilities had already recommenced—if they could be said ever to have ceased — between the Turks and Montenegrins. But, whatever the difficulty, or even danger, no one doubted (in this every Consul was agreed) it would be less hazardous than the

attempt, under present circumstances, to pene-
trate deeper into Albania or Bosnia. They
said that the cry of war had excited a deep,
fanatical hatred against all foreign Christians
in the breast of the common Turk, who fancied
that the present troubles, probably about to
end in their expulsion from Europe, were the
result of the information carried by Frankish
spies concerning the nakedness of the land,
and that a solitary foreigner, even an Englishman, would hardly be safe from violence in
the more secluded, and therefore more grossly
ignorant, parts of the country. The assassination of Christians, even of the richer class,
is unhappily of no very rare occurrence.
Thus, within a year, "a Triestine merchant,
named Salvare, who resided with his family
near Durazzo, was shot dead as he was going
into church on Sunday . . . the only conceiv-
able motive of the crime being a fanatical
hatred of his religion!" So I was assured
by his brother.

Accompanied, therefore, by M. Pericles
Bonatti, the Vice-consul's son,—the father was

infirm,—I ascended by a rocky path the steep
and high hill, on the top of which stands an
ill-repaired and middle-age looking castle, of
considerable extent, at once the residence and
fortress of the Pasha.   Externally, but little
change seems to have taken place in it during
the last four centuries; internally, however,
a lofty minaret tower, with its Muezzin utter-
ing from the little gallery at the top, which he
walks round at the same time, his monotonous
and melancholy call to prayer for mid-day (a
devotion which, like the "Angelus" of the
Catholic Church, is repeated at sunrise and
sunset), and a large, low building, looking
like barracks, but arranged as the rest of the
houses here, indicate that it has been accommodated to the usages of its Turkish masters,
who have possessed it ever since the days of
the last of the Castriotts; *h. e.*, long enough to
compel some alteration, if only perforce of
decay and the ravages of time.   Two rather
ill-looking fellows, in an attempt at uniform,
stood as sentinels at the outer gate, and pre-

sented arms on our approach. Other soldiers
loitered about through the yard in national
costume, which, when complete, imparts a
considerable display of offensive weapons—
long gun, pistols, and hangjar—while a few
dismounted rusty-looking cannon lay around.
In the lobby, or open gallery leading to the
Pasha's divan, lounged a number of swarthy,
fierce, but not very soldier-like men, some in
uniform, others in more or less handsome
national dress. The whole place had a free-
and-easy, barrack-like appearance. In an open
room hard by, whither we went for a few
minutes, sat a venerable old man before a
writing-table. This was the Pasha's treasurer,
an Albanian Christian, who, as far as respect-
able looks go, easily bore the palm amongst
the whole *cortège*. It struck one as remarkable, that that office should be committed to
a Christian, amongst such strict Mussulmans.
On entering the divan we found Osman Pasha,
a civilized-looking gentleman, something above
fifty, seated on one of the sofas, and dressed

in European uniform, with boots so thin they seemed made for sofa wear, though their master did not sit cross-legged either on this occasion. His manners were courteous, and even high-bred. I may observe that he is descended from one of the most ancient families in Bosnia, once, of course, Christian, but long since apostatized to Islamism. His wife, to whom he has been married twenty years, and to whom popular rumour says he is devotedly attached, is of equal birth. Their matrimonial felicity is the more remarkable as they have no children. After the usual pipes and coffee, which were handsomely served in silver by black servants—slaves from Africa—we talked through an Italian dragoman (for the Pasha could not, or would not, condescend to speak any language but Turkish), and I requested permission to pass Lessandrovo, the last of their stations on the lake, on my road to Cetinja, the capital of Montenegro. " It is a little difficult," he replied, " for we are again expecting trouble from those *bestie*"—that, however, at such a crisis as the present, nothing should be refused to an Englishman. Accordingly, his secretary was directed to draw up a firman to the Bey in command on the island of Lessandrovo, to which the Pasha's seal was affixed; and I then took my leave. His Excellency also at the same time broke up his divan, and descended into the neighbouring plain to superintend some artillery practice, which, as well as the distribution of ammunition throughout all the neighbouring villages, was intended, I believe, as a demonstration to intimidate their unquiet neighbours, the Montenegrins, who were suspected of intending a renewal of their raids into the Pashalic.

The rest of the day was spent in a visit to Monsignor Fra Giovanni Topìc, bishop of Alessio and administrator of this diocese, and somewhat later to the Austrian Vice-consul, who spoke French, as well as Italian and German.

The cathedral of Scutari, the residence of so many thousand Christians, during so many centuries, too, stands in a small enclosure of its own, and would, I should think, contain twenty persons standing, certainly not more! On Sunday mornings the poor people crowd into the courtyard, happy if they may obtain a glimpse of the altar. I was assured that hitherto the Turkish authorities would not, on any account, concede more church-room, or allow, even here, any external emblem of the Christian religion.

To those who are descended from the original Christians, the profession of their religion is allowed on payment of a yearly tax, or " tribute," as it is called; but *converts* from Mahometanism are still liable to be punished with death. The same punishment is appointed to be inflicted on those who, after feigning to belong to the established religion, return to the profession of Christianity. This was quite recently exemplified in the case of two peasants, " George and Antonia Craini,"* who stood in the relation of uncle and niece; the

* See "Christians in Albania," quoted above.

former being likewise guardian to the latter, through the premature death of her parents, and who, belonging to the "occult" Christians (*i.e.*, such as believe in Christ, but secretly, to escape the tribute), had been induced, by the exhortations of their bishop, to make open profession of their faith. They likewise hoped that, having paid a bribe of five hundred piastres, which had been accepted, they would escape the legal penalty. The affair, however, got wind, and was immediately taken up by the zealots. Both were seized, placed in irons, and imprisoned, he in the castle, she under the custody of the Zingari, or Gypsies, who in Albania have the charge of female prisoners. The man, after long torture with the tombuk* and scourgings, made a pretended abjuration of Christianity, and was banished to Lessandrovo, to be kept there under surveillance; whence, however, he escaped into Montenegro, and thence proceeding to Cattaro, finally found

* The tombuk is an instrument of torture, in which the sufferer is laid down and weights placed upon his chest, to impede respiration.

a resting-place in Southern Albania, where, being in security, he, of course, renewed his profession of the Christian faith. In the meanwhile, his niece, Antonia, a girl of eighteen, and unmarried, remained in her jail, notwithstanding every effort on the part of the consuls and bishop, by representations to the local governor, and, through the ambassadors, to the authorities at Constantinople, to obtain her release. It was a particularly hard case, since she had been educated in Christianity without any consciousness of the fraud practised by her parents or guardians; and now, though imprisoned for six months, and tried by every species of threat and promise, accompanied with terror, steadfastly refused to renounce her faith. At length, after long suffering on her part, and a course of systematic evasion and shuffling on the part of Osman Pasha and those about him, she was finally liberated by the intervention of Omar Pasha, and allowed to rejoin her uncle amongst the Miriditi, a tribe of free Albanians, to one of whom she was engaged to be married.

VII.

AT seven the following morning I was ready
to depart for Montenegro, and taking leave
of the Vice-Consul proceeded, under the guid-
ance of his son and a dragoman, through
the town to the bazaar, where it abuts upon
the waterside, that is, the river already mentioned, a few hundred yards from the lake,
which is its source of supply. Here we learnt
that no "Londra" (so they call their boats)
was going until the afternoon. This was tire-
some. First, it would entail another night on
the road to Cetinja, the first place where I
could hope to obtain decent accommodation.
Secondly, the bazaar contained nothing but
stalls or open shops,—those who kept them

living at a distance in the city,—and scarcely afforded a place of refreshment where one could get a dinner on the humblest scale. At length, towards one o'clock, the dragoman succeeded so far as to procure me a couple of small fried coarse fish—from the lake—at a cook's shop, on which, and some grapes and bread, purchased elsewhere in the bazaar, I was fain to content myself, not that day only, but the next also, as the event proved.

The intervening time I spent in walking about the bazaar, and at the stall, or shop of the Messrs. Summa, where I was introduced to two of the brothers—handsome young men, something under five-and-twenty, of gentle, amiable manners, and features so finely chiselled as to distinguish them even amongst the Albanesi, whose reputation of being the handsomest of the European races is not at all exaggerated, so far as my experience goes. These brothers in particular reminded one of Vandyke's picture of Charles I., only with a darker, more southern complexion, and an expression softer,

more vivacious, and less melancholy than that
of the Stuart king. Their elder brother, the
principal in the firm, lives at Venice, and has
been lately made a cavaliere by the Pope, in
testimony of the zeal with which the family
have during fifty years received to hospitality
in Venice all the Franciscan fathers going to
and returning from the mission in Albania,
which is entirely served by that order: a
remarkable example for the nineteenth century of the good old virtue of hospitality, and
its acknowledgment! The account of the
state of the Christians in Albania, and their
Turkish masters, already related to me by
the consuls and the clergy at Antivari and
Scutari, was fully confirmed by these brothers,
who seemed well acquainted with the facts
detailed above.

While I was sitting in the cook's shop
at dinner, and expecting the time for the
Londra's departure, my attention was suddenly roused by a disturbance outside. Looking through the unglazed windows, and

inquiring of the bystanders, with the assistance of the dragoman, I learnt that it was occasioned by a stall-keeper, who kept oranges for sale, having fallen upon and beaten a boy, who had ventured to set up a basket of the same fruit in the street nearly opposite, and thus undersell the tradesman. The latter, having in vain warned his competitor to be gone, took a stick, and exercised summary vengeance on him for this, as he considered, no doubt, infringement of his rights. The belaboured boy's resource was to fly from the spot, and invoke the assistance of the Bey of the market-place, or bazaar. Presently came an officer from that official, and entering the stall of the fruiterer ordered him to follow him into the presence of the Bey. The shopkeeper, however, coolly drawing out one of his pistols, told the officer to touch him at his peril, or, if he pleased, to follow him into the open fields where they might fight it out. He then made a hasty retreat over a narrow bridge leading into the country, and left the

M

puzzled officer to return and report progress
to his master, the Bey.

At two o'clock the Londra was ready to
start. It conveyed a small load of charcoal
and eight Turks, four of whom rowed, the
others taking their turns. At first it required
great efforts to stem the rapid current running
from the lake, but, this once passed, it became still water, like other lakes. The evening
was lovely, and during the ensuing four hours
that we rowed on I lay in the bow of the
boat contemplating the scenery on either side,
and the fortress-crowned rock at the end of
the lake, surrounded by its white villas, and
embosomed in orchards, as they gradually
receded from sight. At length, about six P.M.
we turned into shore, by a little square guard-
house, or room, built entirely of wood, and
occupied by a solitary sentry, which stood on
piles, projecting five or six feet above the
surface of the water, within gunshot of the
bank, on which there was another similar
guard-house to correspond. Here, after

answering the sentinel's challenge, the crew prepared to pass the night. This was done by mooring our boat alongside another, into which, as being empty and somewhat more roomy, we transferred ourselves, and, spreading our coats, shawls, or capotes, according as we were provided, first supped, I on the remainder of the bread and grapes from Scutari, they on a much coarser bread, garlic, and Indian corn, and *then* lay down to sleep, "sub dio." In fact it became dark at seven, and there was nothing else to be done. The night was chilly, notwithstanding the warmth of the day, which had been considerable; and it is doubtful how I should have got on, being but slenderly provided with wrappers for sleeping out of doors, had not one of the men during the night thrown over the plaid shawl in which I was lying an Albanian capote, which is perhaps the warmest of national dresses. Nothing indeed could be kinder or more attentive than my Turkish boatmen, who would have willingly shared their supper

with me, if I would have let them. Unfortunately we had no medium of communication.
They understood neither Italian nor Illyrian,
and the only word in their language (*i.e.*
Albanian), which was intelligible to me,
as they talked to one another, was the often
repeated "Shkodra,"* by which ancient
appellation it is still known to its inhabitants.
In short, it is a tongue utterly unlike any
other in Europe.

Soon after five we were again on our feet,
and the Turks, shoving the boat off, rowed
away stoutly. The scenery grew more wild
and beautiful, and the rising sun greatly
enhanced the effect. The long valley, double
the width of the lake, and bending in a half-
moon, was shut in to the east by a lofty
range of mountains, now deeply tinged with
purple light; on the west by the rocky
ground, which rose at once from the water,
and, by reason of our course lying close under
it, shut in the view on that side. On the flat

* So pronounced.

side of the lake, the plain between the water
and the mountains appeared to be quite waste
and untilled, but the steep rock above us
exhibited here and there specks of culture,
a terrace of vines, a few olives, or a bit of
maize, near some rude huts. At the apex of
the lake's southern extremity, the castle on
its exalted base, and the white houses of
Scutari still kept in view. To the north
beetled the dark and savage-looking Crna
Gora.*

Along our path were strewed numerous
little islands, some rocky and barren, and
some quite overgrown with brushwood of
acacia, and pomegranate ; at one of the latter
the men stopped between seven and eight A.M.
to eat their breakfast, while they added to their
stores by gathering a sackful of wild pomegranates, which grew in profusion all over
the island, but were of a rough, bitter sort,
very different from the sweet one I had eaten

* So written, but pronounced Tserna, or rather Tsrna, the
e being dropped or slurred over in Slave.

at Antivari. Then we rowed on again, stop-
ping as often as occasion required at the
islands, which, over and above their pomegranates, were doubtless safer from the long
guns of lurking Montenegrins than the rocky
shore along which we glided at a respectful
distance. Soon after one o'clock, we seemed to
be approaching the opposite end of the lake,
and two islands of more importance appeared
on the broad expanse of waters, both occupied
and one fortified. In the first was a guard
of Turkish soldiers, all in national costume,
sitting or lounging about round their captain,
at the door of their guard-house. The
captain himself sat *à la Turque*, cross-legged,
on a low stool, smoking his pipe, while two
magnificent hounds, of a breed like the Scotch
or Irish staghound, fierce as tigers, and
evidently dangerous to approach, couched at
his feet. The chief, * with the usual good-
breeding of a Turk, invited me to come on

* Who spoke Illyrian, being, most probably, like Osman
Pasha, from Bosnia.

shore, while he made preparations to forward my business. Accordingly I went, and was soon seated by his side drinking black coffee, without sugar, and drawing long whiffs of smoke out of his meerschaum,—a piece of ceremonial good manners which in Turkey must never be omitted. While thus employed, there came a peasant from the Montenegrine side, in a boat, with a pair of ell-long eels to sell—for the lake abounds in fish, as well as leeches of the finest quality. The fisherman asked five grosch, about sixpence English, but presently came down to half the price; for while he was chaffering about it, the two dogs, with looks full of mischief, gradually sidled nearer and nearer to the boat, and in another instant would have sprung into it. The Turks caught hold of them, but the Montenegrin was glad to take what they pleased to give him, and push off. In fact these hounds are kept by the Turks for hunting the Montenegrine highlanders, and forcibly reminded one of the bloodhounds employed to overtake the " children of the mist," in the Legend of Montrose. Presently, a small boat having been got ready, I crossed, with the boatman-in-chief of the crew which brought me from Scutari, and a soldier, over to the larger and fortified island, called Lessandrovo. This, formerly in the hands of the Montenegrins, was taken a few years ago by the Turks, who have held it since; a bey resides in its low-walled fortress, and a small frigate moored close by gives them the command of the lake. The Turks had a fortress also on the mainland, at this end of the lake, close under the mountain of the Montenegrins, called Zhabliach, or Jabliach, but it was surprised, in the spring of 1853, by the latter, who finding they could not keep it without injuring their cause in the public opinion of Europe, by the advice of Russia, burnt and abandoned it. Lessandrovo is now the only strong place on this side of the Montenegrine frontier.

I was not kept long at Lessandrovo. As soon as the bey, who was sitting in his little divan external to the fort, had read with all respect the pasha's firman, he looked around him for some one to execute the commission —not such an easy one, as I found—of sending me over to their enemies. His eye fell upon an African—a " Moro "—to whom a nod intimated his master's wishes. The Black, shrugging his shoulders and looking much " as if he couldn't help it," got up and went with me without any more opposition than the repugnance his face declared, which, to be sure, was not a little. It seems, however, he soon resolved on an expedient for extricating himself from the dilemma and putting me into other hands. Accordingly he ordered my boatman to take us to another island, on which was a neutral Montenegrine village, called Vranin, and which lay within ten minutes' row of Lessandrovo. On the road thither he disclosed to me, in somewhat Nigger Italian, which he had learnt, he said, while in service at Durazzo, his invincible resolution not to go to Ariecca, the Montenegrine port on the lake :

"Mi no vado per niente ad Ariecca, perchè mi tagliano subito!"—It was just three o'clock when we reached Vranin (which had been better called "Pigsty," so horribly filthy was the whole place down to the very water's edge), a village consisting of a few thatched cottages surrounded with fences of maize-straw, with several men and children idling about, and a great lot of pigs, who wallowed in the profound mire. The Black went ashore to provide for my onward journey, I in the meanwhile writing a note to go back with my faithful Turkish boatman to the Vice-consul at Scutari, according to the express wish of the latter, strongly backed by his dragoman, to announce that I had reached thus far in safety. Having received this the Turk rowed off leaving me with the Black, the pigs, and the Montenegrins of Vranin.

Soon came back the Moro to say he could manage nothing at present, but that when the market-boats came in at half-past three or four o'clock, he would try again, and that then he *hoped* I might get ferried across. It was an anxious time; for evidently to sleep at Vranin would have been a bad business, infinitely worse than on the lake, and to eat there simply impossible: whereas it began to seem a long while since I dined on a scanty portion of fish the day before. As to the grapes, which were not two pounds when first bought, and the bread, four little muffins, it barely sufficed for supper last night (to say nothing of breakfast this morning), so that I felt much averse to getting in for another twenty-four hours of it. To get rid of uneasy reflections, I talked to the poor Black, who was evidently a good, honest man, and called forth my sympathy by relating how he had been sold and brought from Egypt to Durazzo, and thence was at length transferred to his present situation amongst savages, "barbari," who were continually thirsting for the blood of himself and those around him—no exaggeration, it must be owned. Though apparently, by his dress, the slave of a master not rolling in

wealth, he positively refused to be rewarded
for his services, and was scrupulous in making
what he thought a just bargain with the
neutral Montenegrins, who were to convey
me onwards. These were two young women,
who just about four P.M. arrived in one of
many boats laden with fish, brushwood, and
provender for cattle.

The arrangements were soon concluded.
They chose the smallest of the boats, a little
narrow skiff, both ends alike, and half full of
water, which, moreover, demanded the utmost
preciseness of " trimming " to avoid a capsize.
In this the Black laid some big stones, on the
stones my bag; and on the bag he deposited
me, high and dry; and then, the women
being perched, each with a little oar, fore and
aft, he wished me " Godspeed," and shoved us
off. I thanked him much, and indeed parted
with the poor fellow with regret under the
circumstances, not expecting to meet anything
half so honest where I was going, or indeed,
often, elsewhere. As to the women, the one

in the bow rowed, the other in the stern steered; they were young and slight-made persons, but of immense prowess, for the boat flew along clearing the water like a light Thames wherry; yet there was only one little oar employed in the work of progression, for the second contented herself with keeping the head of the boat straight. They were, as I said, young ; they were also good-looking, with small, regular, Grecian features : the one who rowed could not have been eighteen; the other, five or six years older, would have been eminently handsome had it not been for a certain fierce Montenegrine expression, much enhanced, perhaps produced, by numerous scratches on one cheek, which looked as if she was not unused to fight the battles of her country, or perhaps occasionally engage in a private duello of her own, to keep herself in practice during times of public peace.

However this might be, their behaviour was highly decorous on the present occasion; yet what a striking contrast to that of the Turks I travelled with a few days since!—such a free, unconcerned bearing as they sat talking to one another across the boat. It brought forcibly before one the totally different position of the *women* in the two countries. Their dress was a simple long white flowing "camicia," girded with the characteristic black sash of the Monte Nero; in addition to which the elder wore a broad brass girdle, set full of large red cornelians, looking like a number of old-fashioned seals. Though both were married, as I afterwards learned, the elder played the part of a careful chaperon to the younger, reminding her as often as her dress became the least disarranged with the exertion of rowing, which, to be sure, was not unnecessary, for apparently beneath the aforesaid white robe there were no extra petticoats. Such, then, was my cortège.

I said it was about four, P.M. when we left Vranin; in an hour or so I had been led to believe we should easily reach Ariecca, and we glided along so smoothly and so swiftly, and the lake seemed so near its termination, that at first I was beguiled with the fond hope of arriving without difficulty by daylight. But the evening drew on; it got darker and darker, both from the approach of night, and the increasing shadows of the gloomy mountains, which rose up steep and precipitous from the water's edge; and yet on we went, across meers, through fields of thick sedges in which there was no opening until we made one, and then, as the lake narrowed up into a corner, round abrupt angles of vast, massive rocks towering above our heads, up gullies, and at length into a long, narrow inlet (or estuary, as it eventually proved to be), the end of which the eye could not reach. One, two, almost three hours passed away, and still no appearance at the extent of vision of any town or village, or houses of any sort; that is to say, of lights denoting their whereabouts, for it was now quite dark. Of people, when we saw any during daylight, whether in boats or on the shore, we had kept clear, as the weaker party; but now loud, noisy, jeering voices (a great contrast to the silent Turks) were often heard close to us in the dark. Once,—but that was earlier in the evening, while we were yet in the sedge-fields,—we passed close by a boat of armed Montenegrins, who had been fishing and shooting wild fowl, which they offered for sale ; and again, about the same time or a little after, as we rowed by a hamlet on the shore, a man's voice demanded in a disagreeable tone, "who I was and whither going?" I replied without hesitation, "A stranger from Scutari, going to Cetinja to visit the Archimandrite," which seemed to satisfy him. Soon after, suddenly, my fair companions stopped their rowing, and abruptly declined to go any farther unless they were paid. Of course, this was not to be thought of with persons of whom I knew so little, except that they belonged to a nation of somewhat doubtful character for honesty.* Neither did I feel myself altogether in their power. Whatever might be their prowess

---

* It is to be observed that I have not a word to say against the personal honesty of the Montenegrins, whose behaviour to me, during my short sojourn, was marked with uniform kindness. It is to their national character amongst their neighbours, as marauders, to which allusion is made in the text.

elsewhere, just where we were I had the best of it. They had told me before that they could not swim : now, the edge of the boat was so nearly on a level with the water in which it floated that perfect unanimity on board was indispensable to *their* safety ! So I gently, but decidedly, declined paying the fare here, or indeed anywhere else, until we reached Ariecca ; adding that, once there, if contented with them, I had not the least objection to pay double the sum for which I had engaged through the African. With this understanding we went on amicably; and at length, about an hour after nightfall, lights in the distance announced the vicinity of human habitations. A little longer, and the boat ran lightly upon the beach.

The night was very dark ; and, as there were no sounds of anyone stirring, I sent up one of the women first to announce my arrival in the dominions of Prince Daniel, lest, as my friend the Black hinted, these people, his subjects, being given to summary proceedings towards Turks, should take it into their heads to make no difference in their treatment of the Turks' allies, in which light, of course, as an Englishman, I might expect to be regarded. As she never returned, I was fain to set off myself for the chance of being allowed to tell my own tale, previous to decapitation, at least. So, getting out of the boat, I was soon up from the shore into the street; when I was at once attracted to a cottage, with an open door showing a blazing light within, which looked hospitable, and not in my circumstances otherwise than inviting. Inside were both men and women making the best preparation their certainly *scanty* means allowed of to receive a visitor, and who, on my showing myself, instead of endeavouring to shorten me by the head, after the pattern of the Black's fears for himself, came forward with the heartiest and warmest welcome, as if they had known me half-a-dozen years at least, brought in your humble servant, set him beside the hole in the floor, out of which the fire was so comfortably blazing, and proceeded to prepare some supper, such as it was : coarse maize bread, and cheese, besides a lump of pork and some eggs, which latter were roasted in the said hole.

In the meantime my fair comrades of the boat came in, and several neighbours (to all of whom I appeared to be an object of no slight interest and curiosity); and we all sat upon low stools round the fire, from which an old woman, seating herself at my side, elicited bright flames by poking in strips of pine or birch, and then holding them aloft for the minute or two they lasted, to light the way to our mouths, as the saying is. As to the smoke, it ascended up through the midst of us, and, after wandering about in the rafters for a while, got out somewhere without benefit of chimney, of which there was none; nay, nor any window, except after the *most* primitive pattern.

Presently, as if to lighten the task of conversation,—for in Slave I was not then very much *au fait*, besides Montenegrine being a new dialect to me,—they fetched in a Scutarine leech-merchant, who also spoke Italian, and was a person of superior education (in Ariecca, that is) : in fact he was a stranger, like myself, but staying here to sell his wares. He addressed me very courteously, and began lamenting the badness of the fare which I had to put up with, especially the Turkish corn or maize-bread, which in these parts is in universal use, insomuch that he designated it as *their* bread, as contradistinguished from *mine*, that is, people's elsewhere. He gave a good account of accommodation at Cetinja, which he spoke of as a wonderful capital, and where I, "Lei," should get " il suo pan "—*my*, *h. e.* "wheaten bread." But, to own the truth, I was so tired of fasting, having eaten nothing but a very little plate of fish and a few grapes in two days of hardish work, that I did not stop to consider what bread it was, though no doubt I should have preferred *wheat*-bread, had it been there. His good manners, however, I am sorry to say, ceased with the Italian, which he addressed only to me; directly he relapsed into Slave, and spoke to the others, he was as rude, free, and jeering as the rest, and diverted himself especially with coarse jokes upon my guides, which piece of bad breeding, however, he assured me next morning ought not to be detrimental to my good opinion of the parties, since it was only in compliance with *their* national customs!

Next we prepared to sleep: beds were spread upon the floor opposite one another; here, for me; there, for my *compagnes de voyage;* another for an old man, &c., &c.; another for the merchant.

Wrapping myself up as completely as I could against vermin, and intensely tired, I was soon sound asleep. How long my slumbers lasted I cannot precisely say; what put an end to them I will not attempt to describe particularly. Suffice it for all purposes

" . . . . . . that great was the smart.
I first dreamt I was dreaming, and then with a start
I awoke, and I rubbed my eyes.
I had dozed, dear Felina, with *thee* on my breast."

In a word, by the gray light of the morn,
I suddenly became cognisant of a large society
besides that described above. Imprimis, a
cat and her kittens were endeavouring to make
themselves at home upon my chest; numerous
fowls occupied the blackened rafters above;
a big pig snored in a corner under a table;
while mice and fleas innumerable gambolled
freely! Notwithstanding, by virtue of some
violent plunges, I managed to get free from
all my tormentors, and was actually going to
sleep—so fatiguing had the two last days been,
—again ; nay, I was already dreaming, in spite
of disagreeable company, and the grunting
of the "porco," who, I confess, disturbed me
far the worst of the whole, when of a sudden
his proceedings became more intolerable than
ever. Just as it began to dawn, he was on
his legs, drawing nearer and nearer to where
we lay,—on the ground, please to observe,—

and evidently in quest of something to eat. What was to hinder his taking off one's nose and cheek at a bite! What an ignominious mutilation! Probably something similar occurred to the minds of my neighbours, for we all sang out at him as he approached our respective beds, and, being sleepy too, each in his native idiom : "Via porco," cried the Italian ; " Bezhi kermach," roared the Slaves ; " Heigh, pig," shouted I, each to his momentary dismay, and happily temporary irresolution. Then we all joined in chorus together to his utter discomfiture, and, some one at the same time most opportunely opening the door of the tenement, out he rushed to my infinite joy! The rest were minor evils ; besides, it was now morning; we got up and shook ourselves,—that was our toilet,—and forthwith felt fit for anything!

VIII.

ARIECCA—CETINJA—MONTENEGRO AND THE MONTEGRINS —CATTARO.

THE streets of Ariecca—positively there are streets—are colonnaded on either side, for the convenience of vendors, who thus set out their wares in a sort of covered bazaar, while the centre, which is left for passengers, whether on horse or foot, partakes of the character of a prolonged dunghill—at least *did* so at this season of the year, being, no less than Vranin, strewed thickly with maize-straw, which rain and the passage of four-footed animals had mashed into the ordinary state of a dirty farm-yard.

Being obliged to wait an hour or more for the mule which was to carry me to Cetinja,*

* Or Tsetinja.

I was traversing these streets attended by
an intelligent, but somewhat saucy-looking
boy, of about thirteen, who was to be my
onward guide, when the leech-merchant of last
night hailed me from his alcove, and invited me
to sit down on his carpet—for everyone in these
parts has a carpet, and more or less imitates
the Turkish divan.   I complied for a while to
ask him some questions, to which he replied
with the frankness and courtesy of yesterday.
He was selling ready-made clothes, which he
embroidered to suit the Montenegrine costume, and large variegated leeches, which he
said came from the marshes bordering on the
lake, and are sold at Scutari for from eight to
ten shillings per thousand.   There was a book
lying by his side on the carpet, which I
opened and found to be a volume of the
" Cerbske Narodne Pjesme," a collection of
the national Servian ballads, &c., by Vuk
Stephanovíc, printed in the Cyrillish character
some years ago at Vienna.   I asked the boy
if he could read, and he immediately took up

the book and began chanting it with great fluency in a low, monotonous tone, so as to leave no doubt that it was a very popular work, and regarded as national here no less than in Servia; for, indeed, the Servians and Montenegrins are the same race, and, though separated under two distinct governments, are yet closely allied in feeling, religion, and dialect. The boy, I found from subsequent conversation, was intended for a "pope," or priest.

Returning to my "hotel" to prepare for departure, which ensued about nine A.M., mine hostess, to whose kind attention I owed various minor comforts, which I can have no doubt are reckoned articles of luxury and *hyper*-refinement in Ariecca, such as, soap and clean water to wash with, and a towel to dry oneself withal, and the like,—my hostess, I say, asked me, but delicately, through a third party, if I would sell her my shepherd's plaid, which, to be sure, singularly enough displayed the Montenegrine colours, white and black. I was, however, obliged, for various reasons, to decline parting with so necessary an article of clothing; but I excused myself to her on the single plea that it was a gift from a friend before I left home, and against my honour to return without it, otherwise I should certainly have begged her acceptance of it: a reply which she appeared quite to appreciate.

Soon after, bestriding a mule, I quitted Ariecca, and, accompanied by the already mentioned boy, sped up the rugged and steep ascent to the little table-land and oval plain of Cetinja, a journey of about five hours. There was little or no cultivation on the road. How could there be? It is throughout a bed of stones, a mere continuation, geologically, of the stony Carst and rocky shores of Dalmatia, with the simple addition of greater height, inaccessibility, and barren bleakness. Yet here and there we passed a solitary fruit-tree, and, though rarely, just by where they had stacked an immense heap of stones all round, a little field for Turkish corn, or grass, or even potatoes, which latter become more frequent on the Cattaro side of the mountain. The soil, when turned up, looked black, light, and fertile.

The Montenegrins who met us were all armed much after the fashion of the Turks down in Albania, but with this difference, that from poverty, I suppose, they had but one pistol, whereas the Albanians had always a brace. In short, all their accoutrements betokened a very needy people. Their salutations likewise were characteristic, indicative of the Greek, not Catholic Slave. Fortis, in his " Journey "* in the last century, has a similar remark. Here, amongst the Greek Slaves, we were invariably accosted with "Pomozi Bog,"† " Bog vas pomagao,"‡ " God help," " May God assist you ! " — whereas the Catholic says, " Hvalen bodi Iesus Christus! "§— "Praised be Jesus Christ ! "—the expression

* Cf. Costumi dei Morlacchi.   † In Latin " Deus adjuva !"
‡ " Deusvos adjuvet!"   § "Laudatus sit Iesus Christus !"

which made so much impression on Klopstock the poet, when he heard it for the first time accidentally in Switzerland, that he blamed himself for not knowing by instinct, what he considered the *very* apposite response, "Na večni cas,"* that is, "Amen," or "for ever and ever." The same salutation is in use among the Italians who live bordering on the Slave provinces.

The plain on which Cetinja is built forms an oblong, skirted by a little wood in the horizon. About the centre, but inclining towards the Cattaro side, some dozen white houses cluster around the fortified convent of the Vladikas, forming what in England would be called a small village or hamlet. In front of the chief building lie a few stones of a more ancient conventual edifice, originally occupied by their episcopal rulers, until it was destroyed by a grand expedition, undertaken against them by the Turks, during a period of intestinal dissension amongst the Montenegrins

* " Per omnia sæcula."

themselves. This was, as we are told by the late learned Vladika, Petro Petrovich,[*] one of the very few occasions when their hereditary enemies of the race of Othman succeeded in getting up here. Neither did they then remain long, being speedily compelled, by the want of all things, to retreat. The other houses are mostly new, of stone, solidly built, and generally two or three stories high. In a word, like other houses in the south of Europe, they seem to have been erected not so much *by* as *for* the inhabitants, to gather them to the spot. Far to the left of the circumscribed landscape is a little white church, with its graveyard, and, behind the convent, on a small hill, a round fort or tower accessible by a ladder only, which was restored lately by the above-named Vladika, and around which, until within the last few months, many Turks' heads were stuck up!

The Archimandrite was not difficult to find.

---

[*] Cf. his "Lazni Car" (or, as we should perhaps better write, Lazhni Czar), "the counterfeit Emperor."

He had rooms in the convent, or *palace*, as it was henceforth to be called, for in fact he was come to perform (temporarily, at least) the spiritual functions of the Vladikas, whose episcopal character has been abolished. My boy-guide hoped to get him to direct his theological studies, and was already well acquainted with the way to his quarters. For myself, acting on his advice, I put up at a tidy little inn, kept by a Cattaran, where I got all that was essential to comfort, or, to come to particulars, a tidy bed-room, a clean bed, and "del *mio* pan."

The afternoon was spent in walking about to survey the place, the Archimandrite undertaking the part of cicerone; and first we turned our steps up to the rough fort or tower mentioned above. The pikes and heads were no longer where, by all accounts, they used to be three or four months back, but strewing the ground beneath; and we trod on many a whitening skull and matted hairy scalp, lying about upon the rocky ground or grassy sward.

The immediate cause of their being thus
roughly removed was the semi-official visit of
a Russian colonel, after Omar Pasha's expedition, in the spring of 1853. He represented it
to the Montenegrins as a specimen of domestic
manners not well calculated to raise them in the
estimation of the other nations of Christendom
in the nineteenth century! The Archimandrite,
however, hastened to make the observation,
that the heads which used to stand there, and
parts of which we still saw below, were none
of the fruits of the late war ("for then," said
he, "the place would have been covered with
them, about three thousand Turks having
fallen on that occasion, though not above two
hundred Montenegrins),"* but of the forays

---

* This has the appearance of a Russian bulletin. But
there would naturally be a great disparity between the
numbers killed in the ranks of the Turks, who were the
attacking party, and of the Montenegrins, who were only
defending their native fastnesses, and mostly fighting behind
rocks. I heard, on *Austrian* authority, that after the Turks
had withdrawn, their *horses* were sold very cheap, in Cattaro
and elsewhere. Turkish colours also were displayed as
trophies, in Cetinja, and even used as coverings for the hay-
ricks, against the weather, in the country around.

before the war began, when never three weeks
elapsed without some one or more Turks' heads
being brought in by the sacking and marauding parties, who, after marching with their
spoils affixed on pikes all about the place
in triumph, finally set them up here as lasting
trophies. He admitted the extreme barbarism
of all this, but at the same time seemed to
think great allowance due in consideration of
the treatment they had received from the
Turks, both, in particular of late years—having
been singled out for special vengeance on
account of their stubborn resistance—and, in
common with the rest of the Christian subjects
of the old Greek Empire, during above four
hundred years. And he instanced, as a specimen of the way in which they used Montenegrins who fell into their hands, their treatment of the Vojvoda, or captain of Grahovo,
when, after a valiant defence, he *surrendered*
during the war last winter, and who, instead
of being regarded as a prisoner of war, or even
tried by court-martial, nay, or without trial

led to *military* execution, was brutally thrown
down and trampled upon until he died—a
cruel and ignominious death for a brave soldier ! Such, he said, had ever-been the style
of usage they had met with from their Turkish
(would-be) tyrants. Originally an offshoot of
Servia, when the Mussulman conquerors overran the rest of the land, they had retreated hither
under their bishop, built themselves huts, and
fortified a convent for his residence. Thus
they had maintained themselves in freedom
ever since, though living the life of wild goats,
on barren and inaccessible mountains, and
descending only for rapine or revenge, and
the purchase of necessary articles in the
bazaar of Cattaro, &c.

Our next point was the residence of the
Vladikas.

The second convent, viz., that which is now
standing and undergoing alterations to make
it more suitable to the altered circumstances
of the ruler of Montenegro, is a plain stone
building, containing a court within the first

or external wall, around which runs a balcony supported on round stone arches. It has a chapel under its roof in which the rites of the Greek-Slave Church are celebrated, but is in all respects as plain and free from any kind of ornament as the most rigid Presbyterian could desire. The Vladikas have been wont of late years to go to St. Petersburgh to receive consecration; but on the death of the last, the renowned and learned " George Peter Petrovich," a change was concerted there, and his nephew, Prince Daniel, to whom the right of succession belonged, declared a secular prince, and sent back to his country with the countenance of the Czar to commence a new reign. Threatened by the victorious arms of Omar Pasha, his reign was well-nigh crushed in the bud; but, escaping by extraordinary good fortune from this danger, acknowledged by two of the great Powers, and decorated with Russian and Austrian orders, he is endeavouring to carry out the contemplated reforms in his small dominions. Plundering expeditions are prohibited, the trial of offences regulated by the Senate and its President, the conscription, a mode of civilization more consistent with the ideas of a Russian than an Englishman, established.[1] In every step he is supported by Russian, and perhaps *Austrian* influence ; and, forasmuch as their forays in time past were prompted by want—so sterile a country being unable to feed its inhabitants —no less than the desire of revenge, his course is rendered smoother by subsidies from both the above-named powers. Thus, *e.g.*, Russia allows him a pension of £4,000 per annum ; while a present of biscuit, accompanied by £1,000 sterling in florins, was on its road from Cattaro, on the part of the Emperor of Austria, the day after my first arrival there. Without some such assistance it is difficult to see how in the present state of affairs the Montenegrins could maintain themselves by any efforts of mere home industry.

The spiritual character of their Vladika, or

ruler, being therefore abolished, the Archimandrite* was at this time chief ecclesiastic
(indeed he was the only person, except his
youthful attendant the deacon, who so much
as wore the dress of the Greek priests).
Whether he was thus to continue, or whether
a bishop would be in time appointed, he professed not to know. "It would depend," he
said, "upon the development of the new
régime." As to the other "popes," or priests,
there was nothing distinctive in their appearance. They wore the national costume as
exhibited on the wealthier laity, and consisting of a dark green or brown, richly-laced
coat, red or black sash, and generally black,
sometimes purple facings. The persons of
highest distinction amongst them had red
cloaks and Polish hussar-jackets trimmed with
fur: probably a Russian cavalry uniform. In
such a red cloak, edged with black ermine,
the Prince Daniel was walking about with

* Archimandrite is Greek for Abbé, or Abbot; from *archi*,
chief, and *mandra*, a monastery.

some of his officers, amongst a crowd of his subjects, who amused themselves with wrestling, leaping, throwing quoits, &c., a gay and lively scene. He is an ordinary-looking, dark young man, of middle stature, about twenty-six years of age, and just about to be married to the daughter of a Triestine merchant, for whose reception the old convent is being modernised. It does not appear that the Vladikas, even when they were *prelates* of the Greek Church, either used any distinctive dress or heard mass with any sort of pomp. On the contrary, they stood in the same national dress as the other priests, and in the usual free-and-easy Greek way amongst the people, unless, that is, of course, they were themselves officiating at the altar. Indeed it would appear from what I heard, no less than from what I observed, that the priestly character was almost sunk in that of the temporal chieftain. The Archimandrite talked as if he hoped that the tone of things would be raised under the new *régime*. He said that the

principality was now for the first time formally
recognised by the two great powers of Austria
and Russia, nay, and acknowledged as independent by the Porte, through the mediation
of the former; that the prince was trying
gradually to infuse more civilised ideas amongst
his people, and to put a stop to brigandage;
that he was having himself taught French, by
a master who was at once a proficient in that
language, as well as in German and Italian,
whom he (the Prince) had brought from
Vienna for the purpose; and that, although
there might be *no schools* at present for his
subjects, he had reason to hope there would
be some eventually under his own (the Archimandrite's) superintendence.

Of course it was natural that the Archimandrite should make the best of the alterations which had been the means of bringing
him to Cetinja, and it must not be forgotten
that Prince Daniel is accused [*] of having
suffered the schools of his uncle, the late

[*] By M. Marnier.

Vladika, to fall into decay. Still one could
not but be glad to hear from any one a
favourable account of the present Prince's
aspirations, since his countenance, it must be
owned, betrayed very small tokens of any
inward cultivation. Materially, there has been
no doubt an advance at Cetinja during the
past two years that his rule has lasted, most
of the better class of houses, including my
little inn, dating since that period. But, notwithstanding their admiration for their late
Vladika's learning and abilities, in which Sir
G. Wilkinson no less than my acquaintance
the Archimandrite appears to have shared,
the mind of the people must be *very low;*
and, to speak more exactly, of that semi-barbarous caste, of which one has examples enough
in the history of the middle ages, or perhaps
even more strikingly in that of the southern
provinces of Austria during the sixteenth and
seventeenth centuries, while their inhabitants
were exposed to the Turkish inroads—a cast
of mind, which in Montenegro has been

retained down to the nineteenth, and which
nothing in the ordinary course of events, but
Christianity acting in unison with civilisation,
can elevate.

Yet for all this we must not lose sight of
the certain fact, that whatever their degrada-
tion in the religious and social scale may be,
they possess broad distinctive marks of superiority over their Mussulman neighbours. One
example of this is apparent in their heroic
struggles against an overwhelming force for
freedom. Another is the difference of their
treatment of the weaker sex. Besides which,
the Turk is under superstitious influences
from which the wildest Montenegrin is free,
and labours under a savage fanaticism, which
presents, as long as it lasts, a hopeless bar to
all progress. Thus during my visit in Albania
every Vice-consul expressed the same appre-
hension from the bigotry of the *Turks* in case
of even an Englishman attempting to travel
amongst them at the present juncture : from
the *Montenegrins*, once safely over the frontier,

no one pretended to say there would be any risk even to an "*ally*" of Turkey. They have the character of being kind and hospitable to travellers, and I have every reason to say that they merit their reputation.

Perhaps this may be a reason for the praise so lavishly bestowed upon them by a class of travellers in these parts, especially of late years. There is, certainly, but little else here to reward the tourist, the lover of fine arts, or of beautiful landscapes. Scarcely in all Europe, could one find a more barren tract, by comparison with which the Carst around Trieste is fertile ; while the journey across the country from Ariecca, with the exception of the tremendous cliffs over which the road runs down to Cattaro, presents an endless succession of crags, and gullies, and table-lands, not stupendous enough to awe, yet quite steep enough to weary, and stony enough to disgust. So long as the rule of their Episcopal Vladikas lasted, there was something mediæval and romantic in the idea of a bishop, politically

independent, living in the midst of his flock
as a temporal, as well as spiritual ruler;
maintaining a strife of ages with unequal
strength, but unabated courage, against the
oppressors of his race and religion—the last
vestige of the independent Slave dynasties,
who were, during so many centuries, dominant
in this part of the peninsula. This military
ecclesiastical *régime*, however, is no more. It
seems to have been regarded by Russia and
Austria as unsuitable to the nineteenth century, and abolished accordingly; nor, looking
to its acts, whether at home or abroad,
without reason; for its forays and bloody
triumphs had been long the scandal and terror
of the whole neighbourhood, not of the Turks
only, but also of the poor Christians of
Albania, and of all the peaceable inhabitants
of the adjacent Austrian dominions, Cattarans
and Ragusans, Bocchesi, and Buduans. The
priestly character of the Vladika, indeed,
seems to have been quite subordinate to the
military; and any one, who came with the

hope of seeing the Oriental rite celebrated with splendour and effect, would have been, at all times, remarkably disappointed; for they seem to have neither the means nor the *animus* for such display, as anyone may judge by comparing their sovereign's chapel with the smallest church or chapel of the poorest Catholic state in Christendom. Even the lover of nationality and admirer of resistance to foreign domination, if he nourished hopes of seeing his ideas realised in miniature at Cetinja, would feel them sadly cramped by the reflection that they are the willing tools of the Russian Autocrat in his views of despotism and schemes of aggrandizement. Their literature (for it must be allowed that, like all other slaves, they have their poetry) is such as might be expected; chiefly devoted to the celebration of marauders, raids, the slaughter of Turks, and the exaltation of the Servians of Montenegro. I must except, however, to some extent, a work I have read since writing the text, by the late Vladika, Peter

Petrovich (already mentioned), which has been published since his death, and consists of an historical drama, entitled "Mali Shtepan," or "The Little Stephen," containing an authentic and interesting account of the adventures and death in Montenegro of that impostor, who, though only in reality a soldier of the imperial guard at St. Petersburgh, contrived to pass himself off, both upon the Turks and the Montenegrins, as Peter III. of Russia, the husband of Catherine, whom she had, in fact, deposed and murdered shortly before (A. D. 1762-4). The Turks sent an army against him into Montenegro, which was repulsed, and, at length, procured his assassination. The Venetians and Ragusans were also amongst his dupes.

Their much-vaunted courage is not undisputed. Certainly, in their night attacks on the unprepared inhabitants of the surrounding districts, their conduct has been the reverse of brave,—nay, much rather, as cowardly as treacherous ; and there are not wanting those

who say of them, as it was said of the Uskoks
of old, that, though very courageous within
stone walls, or behind the shelter of projecting
rocks, in fair fighting they have not, of late,
distinguished themselves.

Notwithstanding all this, in an historical,
nay, and in a political point of view, they are
worth visiting; certainly, they merit attention,
if it were only for the parallel which they
afford with the Uskoks of the sixteenth century. For, in truth, both these nationalities
are witnesses,—first, of the deep-rooted antagonism between Turks and Christians, in
which, as we have seen, both Uskok and Montenegrin have their origin; and secondly, of the
disorganised state of the internal government
of the Ottoman Empire, through whose impo-
tency, Montenegro especially has been enabled
to subsist so long. That the Montenegrins have
no chance of success, either from their own
valour, or from their native rocks, against
disciplined troops, has been proved on two
occasions. Once, early in this century, when

they were repulsed by the French, without
any room left for boasting on their side : and
yet again more decisively, in the spring of
1853, when Omar Pasha had already, in a
very brief campaign, cut off from them the
greater part of their territory, and, with a very
little more time, by the testimony of all,
whether Austrians or Albanians, would have
reduced them to unqualified submission, had
not an extraordinarily wet season caused him
to delay a moment, during which the diplo-
matic intervention of Austria recalled him
from his half-finished expedition.

Thus, then, to the historical student inves-
tigating the fortunes of the southern Slaves,
and their long struggles with the Turks, and
to the political observer of those straws
whose motions indicate the direction of the
brewing storm, Montenegro merits attention,
since, assuredly, it must be an object of
special interest to the Emperor of Russia,
whose religion they profess, whose supremacy, both ecclesiastical and civil, they admit,

whose policy they adopt, and with whose armies they are prepared, on occasions, to co-operate; while, to the traveller for amusement only, whether French or English, Italian or German, Catholic or Protestant, there is very little amongst them to draw forth his sympathies, or to merit an out-of-the-way and troublesome expedition.

No Christian, indeed, can wish that they had fallen, as they were very near on a recent occasion, into the hands of their mortal foes, the Turks, in whose barbarities we find, to a great extent, a sufficient account of their own rise and progress, or, as one would more truly say, *want* of progress, whose former robberies of their territory have reduced them to their present half-starving, uneducated condition, and afford the best excuse for, or at least palliation of, their unsettled life and marauding habits ever since. One could not but deeply regret that any of the essential marks of Christianity, even in a degraded form, should be trodden down under the horse-hoofs of the proud and fanatical Turk.   But one may wish that they may some day find themselves the subjects of a humanising and Christian government, strong enough to put an end to their wild revenges and predatory habits, and benevolent enough to provide for their wants, moral and physical, to promote their civilisation, and, in a word, to care for all their best interests.   There seems to be no reason whatsoever why, if properly managed, they should not turn out just as well as the Uskoks, who were, at least, quite as " *mauvais sujets* " for their time of day, and, in all respects, as difficult a problem for the seventeenth, as the Montenegrins for the nineteenth century.

Early the next day, I mounted, and set out on my return to Cattaro.   The road, just wide enough for two horses to pass one another, led through nearly the same scenery as the day before, first ascending from the plain of Cetinja, then traversing several smaller table-lands of similar shape, until we

P

reached the stupendous precipice, which is traversed by the zig-zag so conspicuous from the sea below. Here it is usual to dismount and walk: no needless precaution, for besides the formidable height, which often goes sheer down, the road is very rough, and the horses, not used to *carry* over it, are apt to trip on the loose stones. Lower down one gets a grand bird's eye view of the Bocche running in, and winding about amongst the minor mountains and lofty banks, which restrain their dark depths beneath. On this side Cetinja were more patches of ground culti- vated than on the other, and the men were working in the little fields amongst their "krumpir" (potatoes) with mattocks, &c., while some reddening woods of oak and beech, though low, scarce, and stunted, gave a little colour to an otherwise cold picture. We passed, latterly, numerous parties of Montene- grins returning from the market or bazaar held to-day at Cattaro, just outside the town, and at last came level with the old castle, which stands on a detached rock above it, once, no doubt, very strong, but now commanded from the zig-zag; finally we reached the dusty little plain, where they were still bartering cattle, clothes, and provender, for man as well as beast, crossed the Fiumara (unlike the deep and rapid Sgorgo of a week ago) a shallow water stealing through a bed of stones, and passed over a wooden drawbridge into the narrow, Venice-like streets of Cattaro.

Here I spent a couple of days, to rest after the fatigues of the week, and then embarked on board a steamer for Trieste.

CONCLUSION.

THE ROAD BACK—SEBENIK—ZARA—TRIESTE.

My "route de retour" was to be accomplished in a steamer coming from Zante and Corfù, which stopped for passengers off the Lazaretto at Megline, where the last little bay or gulf of the Bocche washes the walls of the once strongly-fortified Hungarian town of Castel Nuovo, about four hours' row from Cattaro.

The well-omened vessel destined to convey us to Trieste was ycleped the *Aquila,* and was of greater power, size, and dignity than the Dalmatian boats by which I came in the opposite direction a few weeks before. But it proved a slow-paced bird, and unworthy of its name. It had, however, this

superiority over the other steamers—to a
traveller like myself, hastening to get back
over a line of country already seen,—that
it stopped at fewer intermediate places, per-
forming the whole voyage in five days. I
should also mention that it was more roomy
both above and below deck; but this it
needed, for we had many more passengers,—
Italians, Germans, Dalmatians, Greeks, and
Albanians. In addition, the forecastle and
main-deck were crowded with various de-
tachments of soldiers, which seem, on some
mysterious rule of the Austrian government,
to be continually shifted up and down the
coast. A few companies from Cattaro were
going to Spalato, or Sebenik; there they
gave place to different uniforms and new
faces, which were duly disembarked at Zara,
whence as many as ever it was possible to
stow away above deck and below were
shipped for Trieste.

Amongst the rest of the passengers I soon
recognised my old acquaintance the captain

of artillery, who, having been down in the opposite direction, was now returning on his road to Lombardy. He gave me a kindly welcome, which was all the more appreciable since his political antipathies to my fatherland were not the least abated since we last met. Not that he expressed them to me,—he was far too well-bred to broach the subject, and, for myself, I was not disposed to enter upon politics. But the excitement of the impending war having effectually broken through the usual Austrian reserve on that topic, I heard him inveighing to every one else against "the falseness of our old allies, the insulters of Haynau, the abettors of revolutionists, the harbourers of assassins, and talking of" Messieurs Pa'merstoon, Roossell, and Kossoot" in tones not to be mistaken.

Besides him, there were two Religious, viz., a quiet old Franciscan, in spectacles, and a lively young Jesuit Father, who did not the least require them,—an Albanian merchant from Durazzo, whose brother had been lately treacherously murdered by a Turk, as mentioned above; a professor from the public schools at Spalato, where he first came on board in company with a simple Dalmatian gentleman, who was going, probably for the first time in his life, to Trieste; a young *employé*, in a neat, gentlemanlike uniform, with his bride—to whom he had been married at an early hour the morning he came on board and was going to take possession of 15*l.* a-year salary! as government schoolmaster at Arbe (they were put on shore, however, at Zara, for a brief honeymoon—our steamer not touching at their future home);—these, and some Dalmatian ladies, with divers Slaves, and Greeks in all sorts of national costumes, completed our live cargo. The Jesuit, while he remained, was the life of the whole party. He knew all the coast up and down Albania, Dalmatia, Greece, and Italy, and appeared quite at home in Venice, Trieste, Padua, Verona, Milan, Florence, and Rome. He had such capital stories for the captain and mates that he made them laugh fit to kill themselves, and then embraced them all round with great decorum, but so comical an effect, that he convulsed those who did *not*, no less than those who *did* hear what he said. Next he distributed relics from the Santa Casa, at Loretto, to the ladies, sacred "immagini" (*i. e.* prints) to the sailors, suddenly popped upon me with a question, which quite over-threw my comfortable idea of the incognito of a stranger far from home, and, in a word, exhibited enough knowledge of us all, and versatility to please, to have frightened a very moderate member of Exeter Hall into the belief that he had seen something a great deal more than he ought. To our infinite regret, however, he soon left us, going ashore at one of the towns to give some sacred exercises, or, in other words, to preach a course of sermons, so that, after the first day, we saw him no more.

The other Religious, the Franciscan father, was his antipodes. Like many of his order

whom one meets off this coast, he was from
the mission in Albania, where he had spent
twenty-two of the best years of his life, in
a retired parish of the ancient diocese of
Scutari, preaching the gospel to the poor
Christians of that country scattered amongst
the Turks. At length he was returning,
being recalled to head-quarters. His ex-
periences were interesting, but to record his
picture of the state of things there,—
more suitable, one would have thought, to
ancient Epirus 2,000 years ago, than to
a part of Europe in the civilized nineteenth
century!—would be too much a repetition of
what has been already said.

It is a general characteristic of people who
have not been much from home, nor otherwise
realized geographical distances, to have very
indefinite ideas of the extent of the world;
added to which, the Dalmatians in particular
have a great idea, as it appears, of the travelling propensities of the English. Thus alone,
at least, I can account for the surprise expressed

by a lady of Cattaro, in whose house I was most hospitably entertained on my second visit, that I should never have made the acquaintance of her son, who was living in California! Her amazement, however, received some illustration in the astonishment of the professor's companion, the gentleman from Spalato, who, happening to have met me there as I went down the coast, a few weeks since, now, on seeing me returning in the opposite direction, never doubted that such was my ordinary manner of life whilst abroad. Imbued with this idea, as I presently discovered, he had the curiosity to make out, moreover, how long my last fit of fidgets had lasted. So he took an opportunity, while I was talking to his friend the professor, to ask me, with some slight air of pomposity :—

"Quanto tempo è la V. S. fuori di Londra ? " *

"Cinque anni,"† said I, not divining his drift.

* "How long is it, sir, since you left London ? "
† "Five years."

" No ! " said he amazedly.

" E vero ! " * I repeated, and away he went talking to himself :—" Cinque anni percorso il mondo ! Cinque anni ! Cospetto di Bacco ! "† He seemed to think he had found a cousin-german of the man with the cork leg, or " perpetuum mobile " itself !

Sunday morning we were off Sebenik, having lain in the harbour all night. At six A.M. the steamer would sail for Zara ; but at five, the old Franciscan went ashore to say mass at the church of his order, and I, learning his intention the evening before, begged permission to accompany him. The church was already crowded with people, and blazing with wax candles. Mass was said, as usual in the *towns* on this coast, in *Latin*, only the Epistle and Gospel being read in the vulgar tongue, *i. e.* Illyrian, as elsewhere, to the people, who accompanied the rest of the service with

* " Yes, indeed."

† " He has been travelling about the world for five years ! Five years ! My stars ! "

their voices, singing a national air of a soft melancholy cast, such as the Slaves generally delight in. In the *country* and *villages* where the population all speak Slave, mass is ordinarily said in *Illyrian*, in which tongue the priests also read the Breviary—both the Missal and the Breviary which they say having been translated as early as the times of SS. Cyril and Methodius, who, about A.D. 870, converted their still heathen countrymen. In the great towns, where the population is Italian, this "use," which is now said to be on the decline everywhere, was never adopted. In Venice, however, a few years since at least, mass was thus said in Slave every day, in the church called "Zobenigo;" and *occasionally* at the chapel of the "Scuola Slavonica," one of the celebrated old confraternities, established for the benefit of the Dalmatian and Istrian subjects of the Republic.

On our return to the steamer we were soon again under weigh. The morning was fine, and all looked cheerful, except the artillery officer, who stood so unusually silent, that I hastened to ask him how he had slept.

"Sehr schlecht," * was his reply.

"Ah! no doubt you too found it hot and close," I observed.

"Not at all that," said he.

"How was it, then?" I inquired.

"Why," said he, "in these steamers, there is nothing regular — 'nichts ordentlich' — people getting up or going to bed all night!"

Now I began to feel myself aimed at, for I remembered that he slept, or should have slept, in the cabin next to mine, where I certainly imagined I had heard him snoring, when I came to bed at half-past ten or eleven the night before.

"I will tell you," continued he, "I heard *you* go to bed and get up!"

"And you did not sleep between whiles?"

"Ja!" said he, indignantly; "but what of that? I was disturbed *twice;* and when I

* "Very badly."

am at home, I make but one sleep of it from eight till six."

This was quite too much. "My dear sir," said I, "I beg your pardon. Excuse my ignorance of military life. I have indeed heard as the dictum of a certain great English commander, which always struck me—like all he said—as having peculiar weight, that 'when a man turns in bed it is time to turn out,' but I never knew before that it was a further perfection not to make the fatal turn for ten hours!"

We reached Zara. One more such "irregular" night in our berths, and we should be at Trieste; and a great relief it would be to *me*, though for different reasons from my companion last mentioned, to find myself there on "terra firma" again: for even a few nights on board ship are irksome to a landsman. I was therefore enjoying the thought as I sat at dinner in the *restaurant* room of an inn at Zara, and little reflecting that "there's many a slip 'twixt the cup and the lip," when suddenly a paper is put into my hand by a man in uniform! I hastily read it, and see to my astonishment that my presence at the police-office is required without delay after dinner. What can it mean? Passport *en règle*,—conduct, so I flattered myself, unexceptionable,—recommended by private letters to people in authority, both lay and ecclesiastical,—the only persons I had talked to on the way priests, professors, or officers. These people must be *very* particular, I thought, to except to such inoffensive behaviour. So saying to myself, I walked into the "polizia," and knocked at a door over which was written in German characters, "Ober-Commissär." The official within received me with solemn politeness, doffing his little black cap—a most essential part of the insignia of an Austrian *employé*—and begging me to be seated. I complied. He took out my passport, and began by remarking that it had no personal description of the bearer. I reminded him that English passports never had; on which he proceeded to make one, with extraordinary minuteness. This ended, he closed the book, and begged to know why I came into Dalmatia just *now?* Hereupon I began to descant upon the interest of Roman remains, of medieval republics, of beautiful scenery, of national costumes, and of the autumn being better in the opinion of most tourists than the spring for travel. When I ceased, he looked puzzled how to proceed. At length, after a pause, he said, "But have you not been making remarks relative to the defences of Cattaro when you were in the Bocche?"

"I should rather think not," said I.

"Come, now, to be frank," said he, (seeing there was no coming to the point otherwise,) "I am positively informed that you have been asking such questions as these:—How many men it would take to blockade Cattaro, and how long it would require for a steamer to come from Corfù."

This was really too silly. I laughed outright.

"The fact is," he added, "I have received a letter informing me that you are a political emissary of ——"

"Caro Signore," said I, "there never was so great a blunder. I never had to do with politics in my life. I do remember now once to have observed in mixed society lately that the defences of Cattaro seemed, to my inexperience, insecure, *not*, however, against English mariners from below, but Montenegrins from above. I assure you, I have no hostile design against Austria, in which country I have now resided several years in great peace and friendship with my neighbours; and whatever my political predilections may be,—for of course, after all, I am an Englishman,—I should not broach them amongst strangers so far from home."

This appeared quite to satisfy him; he begged my pardon for the interruption, and we parted on the most friendly terms.

After this I reached Trieste without further adventure; all that I heard about this part of

Q

my travels being from the good-natured prefect of police at Trieste, who, when he saw my portrait in full on the passport, exclaimed, "Aha, signore, va fuora *solo* e cade in sospetto."*

But *some* people *in Dalmatia* were not so easily satisfied; for about two months afterwards, the local governor of the town where I was residing told me, laughing, he had received a letter on the subject, in which his correspondent insisted upon it that I *must* be a political spy, and, more particularly, an emissary of Lord Palmerston's, for that I had gone about the country everywhere making annotations with a book and a thermometer !

* "Aha! sir, you go travelling *alone*, and fall under suspicion."

HISTORICAL SKETCH

OF

THE REPUBLIC OF RAGUSA,

FROM THE

EARLIEST TIMES DOWN TO ITS FINAL FALL.

INTRODUCTION.

The Republic of Ragusa will at all times enter into the province of European history as a state which, though small, was wealthy and independent, and of maritime importance disproportioned to its size; which lasted, in the midst of hostile and semi-barbarous nations, through eleven centuries, itself an emporium of commerce and letters, and a link in that chain which, stretching through the dark and middle ages, connects the great divisions of the Roman empire with our own times. But it becomes yet more interesting in the present day from its contiguity to, and ancient connexion with, that broad and rich territory on whose destiny the eyes of Europe are once more turned, from whose provinces it for many centuries derived its population, and for

whose commercial intercourse with the West,
first under the native Slave rulers, and secondly under the house of Othman, it was the
chief, almost the only outlet. The little that
is known of those Dalmatian kingdoms and
Serb dynasties preceding the Turkish invasion
is mainly derived from Ragusan historians
and antiquaries, and the first cultivation of a
Slavonic language by scholars and writers of
genius is due to the government of the Republic, which so early as A.D. 1400 introduced its study into their schools, and whose
sons, two centuries later, imbued with the
lofty religious spirit of the Spaniard and the
refinements of the Italian, composed poems
which it is no injury to compare with the
chef d'œuvres of Tasso and Calderon.   With
this preface we will pass at once to the con-
siderations which best explain the rise, prosperity, and decay of Ragusa.

There are three circumstances which cannot
fail to strike every one who looks into its history: viz. its remarkable genius for trade, its

undeviating Catholicism, and its school of letters.

The ardour with which the Ragusans applied themselves to commerce is evidenced not only by their widely ramifying treaties with the other nations of Europe, and particularly with the Slave princes, so long as the latter retained their kingdoms; but also, yet more singularly, on the failure of these, by their entering the first of any Christian state into commercial relations with their Mahometan neighbours. At a time when the nations of the West grew pale at the very name of the Osmanlis, and every year added to the terror of their arms; when the fairest provinces of Christendom were trodden down under their victorious horse-hoofs, and the tide of barbarism, sweeping over the frontiers of the present Ottoman empire, devastated Hungary and Poland and southern Austria, and penetrated far into Carinthia and the Frioul before it could be stemmed; when the powerful armaments of Turkish and African corsairs, the Draguts and Vraz Alis, ravaged the coasts of the Adriatic, Sicily, and Italy itself, so that before the battle of Lepanto no part of the Mediterranean could reckon itself safe;—at such an epoch, the boldness of a small Christian state on those very shores, venturing to make peace with the Ottoman power, much more, to enter into friendly connexions with it, for their mutual advantage, was undoubtedly a striking phenomenon, especially when we take into consideration that states did not then, as now, profess religious liberalism, but were as exclusive in their religious profession and toleration as individuals; and that, above all, Ragusa was undeviatingly Catholic; that it preserved at the same time its relations with the other Christian powers, and did not lose their respect; that, in a word, its peculiar principle of conduct forfeited neither the friendship of Europe nor the approbation of the Pope.

Furthermore, its capability of adopting and adhering to a line of policy so novel and so intricate, yet in the main so successful, indicates no small command of political genius. For the men who could venture to guide the helm of State along this path, so narrow, yet so necessary to the preservation of their commonwealth, must have been endued with a firmness, and perseverance, and energy entitled to command our respect; and we feel sure, even beforehand, they could not have succeeded as they did, unless they had possessed gifts of intellect and mental culture commensurate with that moral courage with which they were animated. Hence the philosophical observer of past events, no less than the mere historical antiquarian, will not find it uninteresting to inquire briefly into the system, which during many ages never failed to produce talent and energy to meet the emergencies of a combination so unusual, and a position so arduous.

But such an inquiry, although it need not necessarily lead us into all the minuter details of the history of Ragusa, will not be satisfactory unless it embrace at least some account of its rise and fall; its form of government; the alternate extension and decline of its land and maritime commerce, the flights of its literature, especially its Slave poetry, with a brief enumeration of some of its most eminent literati; the services which it rendered to religion; the disasters which predisposed to its ruin, and particularly that crowning calamity which finally obliterated its greatness, and after prosperity so uncommon, proportioned to its size and natural resources, rendered it known throughout the world for its misfortune.

Before commencing, however, it is necessary to say a few words on the sources of information we possess.

In such a society as that of Ragusa in later years, there would not be wanting learned illustrators of the history of their country. Unfortunately this was not the case in the earliest centuries of its existence, and up to the middle of the fifteenth century we should have been left mainly to conjecture and the scanty notices of foreign writers, had it not been for Meletius, a Ragusan of the twelfth century, about whom little is known except that he left a book in Latin verse on " Epidaurus and Ragusa," of small *poetical* merit, but containing many valuable facts and dates, of which the later antiquarians and historians have availed themselves. From the fifteenth to the eighteenth century—from Cervario Tuberone to Giorgi, Cerva, and the Abate Coleti—there is an unbroken chain of native authors, and a mass of interesting documents, which again have been compiled and digested into a regular history, down to the peace of Passarovitz, by Appendini, an Italian Pierist,[*] who being sent to Ragusa to assist in education at the end of the last and the beginning of this century, and having given himself to the study of Illyrian and the antiquities of the city, was engaged by the Senate to write a full history of the Republic, which he has accomplished in two volumes, quarto, and which have since formed the approved and altogether best account, as received by the Ragusans themselves.

[*] " The Scuole-Pie " flourished as an educational institute after the departure of the Jesuits, in the eighteenth and early part of the nineteenth centuries.

As might be expected under such circumstances, his style is nearly that of a panegyrist, and he defends generally those theses which are gratifying to the national pride of his employers. Still he gives us his authorities, and enters into a critical examination of disputed points ; and, as he had ample opportunity of consulting every original document which the various fires and earthquakes had left, as well as printed works, his account is of great value, and generally entitled to confidence.

Of foreign writers, an occasional reference to Ragusan affairs occurs here and there in Valvasor's history of the neighbouring province of Carniola; and Professor Schaferik, in his learned work on the origin of the Slave nations, treats of this city in common with other nurseries of that race. Sir Gardner Wilkinson, in his "Dalmatia and Montenegro," has given a copious account of Ragusa and its history, which is, however, as he tells us, mainly taken from Appendini.

HISTORY OF RAGUSA.

RAGUSA was founded on the rocks, where it at present stands, by Italian fugitives from the Roman towns of Epidaurus and Salonæ, when they were devastated about the middle of the seventh * century, first by the Avares, and shortly afterwards by the Croats. These rocks were called "Dubrava,"† or the "Forest," in the language of the latter, who, becoming from this time forward the inhabitants of the country round about, gave the name of "Dubrownik" to the new city; by which appellation it is known amongst all the Slave nations.

* It is very probable that the rocks began to be inhabited before the seventh century, i.e. in the fifth or third, for even so early the new situation had become eligible, owing to the inroads of barbarian invaders. It became a *town* perhaps, and was *walled round* in the seventh.

† "Dubrava," means literally an oak-forest, from "Dub," an oak.

The Ragusans, supported by the testimony of Constantine Porphyrogenitus, claim the old Peloponnesian emigrants to Epidaurus, in Roman times a " colony," as their direct ancestors, and place the site of the classical town a few miles south of the present city, on the plain of Canale, at the spot which, in consequence of this tradition, bears the name of Alt-Ragusa, where traces of Roman buildings still exist.   A rival claimant * has been set up in the modern Budua, which so far more nearly agrees with the reputed situation of the tombs of Cadmus and Hermione, the mythological colonizers of the territory of the Republic.   But it seems certain, from the identity of names in both towns, no less than from the words of Constantine, that the families of Epidaurus contributed *chiefly* and *amongst the earliest* to the population of Ragusa, although not *exclusively ;†* for the Roman and Italian

* See Arrowsmith's Comparative Atlas.

† Salonæ, especially, which was destroyed about the same time, contributed a portion. On this ground, *inter alia*, the Ragusans, in after years, founded a claim, against Spalato, to the primacy of Dalmatia. See Appendini.

inhabitants of these Provinces, about the
period of which we speak, were on all sides
deserting the inland and less secure abodes,
which they had occupied during the strength
of the Roman government, and seeking refuge
from their barbarian invaders in a few strong
places along the coast, which afterwards during
the supremacy of the Greek emperors formed,
what was then called, " Dalmatia *Romana*,"
to distinguish it from " Dalmatia Barbarica,"
or " *Slavonica*," that is, the country remote
from the sea.

From its earliest days, therefore, Ragusa
was compelled to turn to the sea for support.
On the land side they had nothing to hope,
occupied as it was by the hostile tribes, who
had recently destroyed their mother cities, and
who, engaged in perpetual wars with what
remained of the Roman race and with one
another, neither cultivated the land themselves
nor suffered the Ragusans to do so. Even on
the sea commerce was limited and hazardous;
for not only was the Adriatic infested by the

Saracens, who are stated by the Ragusan
writers to have joined with the Slaves in the
final destruction of Epidaurus, but, in those
unsettled and lawless times, their Narentan
neighbours, the inhabitants of the old Roman
town of Narona,* had betaken themselves to
piracy as their avowed profession. Yet, however uncertain the source of supply, to the sea
they must look for the means of support and
communication with Constantinople, whose
supremacy as Romans, they still acknowledged, and to whom, like distant colonists,
they looked for aid in times of extreme need.
Thus it was that by the ninth century (A.D.
846—866) they had so fortified their city,
that they could sustain a siege of fifteen
months against the Saracens,† and had ships
enough at their disposal to undertake the
transport of the allied Slave princes to the
siege of Bari on the opposite coast, where the

* Narona appears to have been chiefly occupied by Slaves
at this period, though, like Ragusa, originally of Italian origin.
See Schafarik, ubi infra, and Appendini.

† Appendini calls them "Hagarenites from Africa."

enemy had afterwards ensconced themselves, and to the battle on Mount Gargano, which resulted in the total overthrow of the Saracenic host. In this same century (A.D. 830—840), and immediately before these last-mentioned events, a fortunate war with the bans of Trebunia and Zaculmia, whose territory joined the republic's, terminated by a dexterous treaty, threw open all the neighbouring Slave provinces to their commercial enterprise, secured to the market of Ragusa a supply, no longer precarious or niggard, of all the necessaries of life, and directed their energies towards a new scope, viz. the *land* commerce.

Another event of equal importance, but of disputed date — for Appendini places it a hundred and fifty years earlier,—which befell them, probably in this century, was the arrival of Paulimirus, or Belus, king of Bosnia. This Slave prince, the grandson of Radoslav, who had taken refuge in Rome from a domestic revolution, had been educated in a school of

R

civilization far beyond his native country, and, hence, now on his return to his ancestral throne, to which he had been recalled, came to Ragusa with the best dispositions towards its citizens, whose Roman origin and institutions he regarded with the friendly eye of a relative. Many of his followers settled there, and henceforth we find Ragusa the common refuge of those Slave princes and nobles, who were compelled by political disturbances to leave their country, or who sought to end their days in religious tranquillity. And thus it arose that Ragusa, in the course of the next two centuries, became in great measure peopled with Slave families.*

One great impediment to their maritime commerce in these early days lay in the piratical neighbours with whom they were surrounded; but there was a danger to the commonwealth itself, beside which this evil

* Schaferik's "Slawische Alterthümer II." xxxii. 5 (vol. ii. p. 275, Leipsic, 1844). His expression is, "Völlig Slawisirt wurde."

shrank into comparative insignificance. The ambitious Venetian state, of similar origin to themselves, had not only secured its own independence, the great object of Ragusan policy likewise, but was making rapid strides towards empire. Already the inhabitants of Dubrownik had reason to fear its designs, and had entered into alliance with the Narentans, then all powerful at sea, to oppose its further progress in Dalmatia, when a frustrated attempt to surprise Ragusa itself, followed shortly afterwards by the capture of one of their merchantmen by the Venetian navy, and the refusal to restore it, confirmed their fears and obliged them to join the league of Narenta and Greece against their domineering neighbour. Venice was for the time humbled and compelled to submit to the terms of peace dictated to her by the allied fleet at Pola: but, shortly, recovering herself again, she brought the war with the Narentans, who had in the meanwhile quarrelled with the Slave princes and were opposed by the emperor, to a speedy and successful termination. This was accomplished by a fortunate accident. The issue of the contest was still doubtful. The Narentans abounded in strongholds both at sea and land, from which they fought desperately and often successfully; when it chanced that a Ragusan merchantman, which, besides a rich cargo of wax and silver, was convoying over from Apulia forty Narentan youths of the noblest families, was captured at sea by the Venetians. The parents, dreading the treatment of their children as prisoners of war at Venice, forced their chief to conclude peace on terms which surrendered their maritime superiority; and thus a people, who for three hundred years were the terror of the Adriatic, and levied black-mail on the ships of all nations navigating those seas, disappear from the pages of history, and are henceforth only heard of as bucaniers under the piratical names of Almissani, Kacichi, and people of Krajna; while Ragusa, alternately relieved from either danger,

the ambition of Venice and the depredations of the Narentans, at the end of the
tenth century had opened to her industry and
enterprise an exclusive trade with the Slave
provinces by land, and all the shores of the
Mediterranean by sea.

Of how much importance this land-com-
merce with the Slaves was considered in those
days at Venice may be judged by the means
which the Ragusans took to force upon that
state the restitution of their ship captured with
the Narentan youths. For Ragusa, having
already, before the second war began, re-
nounced its league with Narenta in obedience
to the orders of the Greek emperor, contended
that Venice had no claim on their property.
This plea however was rejected, and the senate
refused the Ragusan ambassadors an audience;
whereupon they went into the Piazza of San
Marco, and there proclaimed to the people at
large that all intercourse between the two
states must henceforth cease. The Venetian
merchants, accustomed during nearly two cen-

turies to trade with Slavonia through Ragusa, were dismayed at the prospect of so great a loss, and by their clamours compelled the senate and the doge, Pietro Urseolo, to come to terms. At length they entered into a solemn treaty with the sister republic, by which they engaged themselves to make restitution, to exchange gifts annually, and to send aid to one another in time of war.* It was thus that Ragusa first obtained from Venice an acknowledgment of what she so highly prized, viz. her independence.

But when we speak of the independence of Ragusa, it must be understood to mean, not the independence of a powerful country, but rather of a free town. Such absolute independence as the former it was not to be expected that they could pretend to. The origin of these states, the republics of the

* The *Venetians* undertook to pay fourteen yards (*braccie*) of scarlet cloth yearly, and to send an armed galley to help Ragusa in time of need. The *Ragusans* to send two white horses and three barrels of " Ribolla " wine yearly, to send an armed galley as above, and to open their market to the Venetians.

middle ages, is to be sought, Sismondi tells us,* in the original constitution of the Roman empire. Rome grew to its full proportions as a republic, and although the Roman Augusti afterwards ruled there as absolute monarchs, they still retained the old framework, and governed through the forms of republican institutions. Hence it followed that the absoluteness of the emperor, and the change in the constitution, were more sensibly felt at Rome than elsewhere. In distant and obscure cities people were comparatively little cognisant of what went on in the capital, to which their relations continued unaltered, whether the executive were directed by the emperor, or the consuls and senate. Their local government retained the same municipal type, which they had always had, whether as " Municipia " they had kept under the Roman sway, their own original laws and customs derived from Greece, or Italy; or, as "Colo-

* Histoire des Republiques Italiennes, chap. v. Vol. I. p. 192.

nies," they were modelled after the pattern of republican Rome. Even if they were important enough at any time to receive a chief magistrate from the metropolis, on his departure they would revert to their original self-government with little external change. Hence we find Ragusa, in the earliest years of its existence, a free town, providing by fortifications and separate treaties for its own safety, but acknowledging the supremacy of Constantinople, whither the seat of government had been transferred, and to which it probably once paid tribute in return for the aid which it could thence claim in time of necessity. It is at least certain that this was the original condition of the other towns of Dalmatia, also of Roman origin, to which we find at one time the tribute remitted (circa A.D. 880), by the Emperor Basil, the Macedonian, all except something nominal, in consideration that he was no longer able to defend them against the Slave princes, of whom it became necessary for them to buy peace with an annual sum. Ragusa, it is true, is not enumerated with the other cities in this correspondence, which shows that it was in different circumstances at that period, but surely is not conclusive, as Appendini contends that it never was subject to the same rule.* Thus, then, we can understand the relations which existed between Ragusa and the eastern empire ; and again how it was that in the empire's decrepitude, preparatory to its dissolution, the Ragusans began to look out for other and more efficient protectors. For the one main evil they had to avoid in their peculiar circumstances was the being dragged by their patron into unprofitable and dangerous wars. It was such an occasion which caused them to renounce the protection of the Emperor Emmanuel in the twelfth

* The Ragusan antiquarians and historians, Banduri and Cerva, consider that their city was always quite free, from its foundation on the rocks as "Dubrownik." This probably means that they did not henceforth stand on the same footing as Epidaurus and Salonæ had stood. Perhaps their tribute was remitted earlier than that of the other Italian towns of Dalmatia; but it is not probable that they could have claimed protection without paying for it in some shape or other.

century — not without considerable loss to their commerce, which was thus shut out of Roumelia—and to turn to William the Norman, King of Sicily. For Emmanuel having, contrary to good faith, arrested the Venetian merchants in his dominions, that republic retaliated by making another attempt, though as unsuccessfully as before, on Ragusa. After the death of William, however, they again reverted to Constantinople under the Emperor Isaac Angelo.

But not only did they place themselves under special protectors. It seems to have been their rule to make friendships and alliance, as early as possible, with every potentate, who came into the neighbourhood; a line of policy which, on more occasions than one in their after history, turned out singularly to their advantage. We have seen how, in the times we have been speaking of, they formed an alliance with the Narentan princes. In the same, the tenth century, they sent an embassy to the Emperor of Germany, Otho II., who, after an unsuccessful expedition against Dalmatia and Calabria,* had retired to Rome. It so happened that Otho had once owed his personal safety in an emergency to the assistance of a Ragusan merchant, and he now, therefore, received their proposals with marked favour, promising them the friendship of himself and his successors for ever. Numerous, too, were the Slave princes to whom they afforded an asylum in misfortune. Some they protected during their minority; some they assisted, either by negotiation or arms, to return to their country; others they aggregated to the state, and admitted to all the rights of Ragusan patricians; and, at the end of the eighth century, they sustained a war and siege of seven years' duration, to protect the family of the pious king Radoslavo from the attempts of

* Otho was defeated at Basentello by the united forces of the Greeks and Saracens. Sismondi, Hist. des Repub. Ital. Vol. I. chap. iv. p. 157. A Ragusan merchant is said to have lent him the horse on which he made his escape from his enemies.

his unnatural nephew, Bodino, and his wife, the cruel Jaquinta.

On this occasion they defended the innocent and their benefactors; for the territory along the coast had been ceded to them by King Stephen, an ancestor of that prince, and the islands known of old as the "Elaphites," or Calamota, Di Mezzo, and Giupana, by his immediate predecessor, King Silvester, while Radislavo himself had richly endowed the monastery of Lacroma, besides other acts of pious munificence on their territory, before his death. But at another period, A.D. 1192, we find them according a promise of protection in case of need to their old treacherous enemies, now in adversity, of the house of Nemagna. This family sprang about a century earlier from Dessan, the son of Orosius, a courtier of Draghikna, the then King of Dalmatia. On the death of that monarch he usurped his dominions, and afterwards, to serve his ambitious designs, though catholic by profession, broke with the Church of Rome

and erected the standard of schism. His son
Nemagna followed the example of his father,
and having by a long course of treachery won
large dominions, assumed the title of " Mega
Giupano," or Great Jupan. During many
years they had taken every opportunity of
injuring the catholic Ragusa, and thus rendered themselves utterly unworthy of any
favour from that quarter. Yet, true to their
established maxims of policy, the senate
granted them protection under their changed
circumstances. " Nor could anything," says
the Ragusan historian, " be more calculated
to impress the untutored mind of the Slave
princes, than this act of generosity so contrary
to the baseness of their own conduct; for
never was there a race more immoderately
elated by prosperity, or more depressed and
vile in adversity." Furthermore, this liberal
friendship with members of a schismatic church
gave the Pope opportunity to endeavour
through Ragusa to win them back to unity;
and even after this had failed, the numerous
colonies maintained by the republic formed

the bases of catholic congregations throughout
Slavonia, and in more recent times throughout
the dominions of the Ottoman Porte.

It is too often the case in this world that
those who from the ties of nature and parity
of interests should be the greatest friends
become the worst enemies. Thus it was
with the states of Venice and Ragusa. Both
of Roman origin, both throughout their political existence adherents of the catholic church,
both fugitives from the barbarians who over-
turned the ancient civilization, both nourish-
ing their early life and their future glory
by application to commerce, and both republics of the same aristocratic mould, we
might have expected them to lend each other,
in proportion to their respective powers, every
support against common enemies and in common dangers, even as they were calculated
from kindred ideas and similarity of institutions to influence one another in progress and
mutual advancement. But in spite of all this
it resulted in the most rooted antagonism.

In the ninth and tenth centuries we find

the Ragusans included in the Narentan league from fear of the designs of Venice. In the tenth they chose St. Blaise as their patron, because the priest who revealed a Venetian plot to seize Ragusa by a *coup de main* declared that this saint had appeared to warn him of it.* In the eleventh, the Doge Domenico Contareno, with a numerous fleet having retaken Zara, which had revolted, came on to Ragusa, prepared with materials on board to build a hostile fort on the rival territory; but this also was defeated by the vigilance of the Ragusan spies; as was a further attempt on the city itself in the following—the twelfth century, the plea for which, on the part of Venice, was the bad faith of Ragusa's patron,

---

* On this occasion the Venetians had come with a fleet to attack the Narentans, A.D. 971, but hoping to take Ragusa first by stratagem, they professed friendly intentions, and anchored under Lacroma with part of their fleet, leaving the rest at Gravosa. The following night they attacked the city on both sides at once, from Gravosa by land, from Lacroma by sea. But the Ragusans having had warning lay under arms all night, and were thus enabled to repel them in either direction with great slaughter.

the Greek emperor, who had unjustly detained
Venetian property.

At length, with the thirteenth century,
Ragusa succumbed to Venetian influence.
The history of this was as follows. The
reign of the weak and treacherous Comneni
was at an end, and with it the Greek pro-
tectorate of Ragusa. Constantinople had itself fallen into the hands of the Gallo-Vene-
tian forces. At such a dangerous crisis, and
while the minds of the citizens were suspended
between mistrust and anxiety, Damian Judas,
their count or president—for such was the
title by which the chief magistrate held his
annual office at that time—towards the end
of his year, omitted to summon the great
council for the election of his successor.
Confiding in his talents, wealth, and influence,
and believing, perhaps honestly, that at such
a moment he was more capable than any one
else of guiding the commonwealth through
the difficulties by which it was beset, he
gained over the soldiery to his purpose, com-

mitted the fortresses into the keeping of his friends, and brought over a considerable portion of the discontented patricians to his views; pretending that the divisions of the nobles at home, and the dilemma resulting from the fall of Constantinople abroad, required for the time a dictatorial government, which, having exercised for the common good, he should in due time of himself lay down. But the opposite faction, headed by the family of Bobali, a name of equal rank and consideration with his own, were not thus to be persuaded; and Judas, informed of all their secret counsels, was driven to attempt to arrest the persons of his antagonists. They saved themselves by a hasty flight into Bosnia, and at the end of two years the party of which they had been the most conspicuous members, were persuaded by Pirro Benessa, Damian's son-in-law, to take a strong measure which would at any rate effectually deliver them from *domestic* despotism. Having pointed out to his fellow citizens how bloody would be the

strife, and how uncertain its issue, if they
should attempt to oppose his father-in-law by
open force; how all hopes were precluded by
the fall of the Greek emperor from that
quarter; and how, through the faithless character of the Slave princes it would bring
about a change for the worse rather than the
better, if they relied for help on them; he
proposed to turn to the Venetians themselves,
who, for the reputation of their justice, from
motives of policy, and for the sake of their
commerce with Slavonia, so great a mart of
their home produce, would be forced to
guarantee the lesser republic against a danger,
which, if it should be realized, they could
not but regard as a common evil; and who
being called in as protectors and friends,
would be disarmed from more formidable
attempts on those liberties, which they could
not fail of undermining if they should attack
them in concert with the Slaves. He concluded by undertaking to negotiate such a
treaty at Saint Mark's, through his adherents

and friends there, as should secure the Ragusans in the free exercise of their institutions
and laws, provided only they engaged to
receive a Venetian nobleman as their count.
This engagement, it is to be observed, was
not uncommon in those times, and did not
imply any political vassalage * on the part of
the recipients; but was regarded merely in
the light of a high compliment to the superior
commonwealth.† Thus, at another period the
Ragusans themselves sent counts to Trau and
Fiume, over which townships, at the same
time, they never pretended to any sovereign
rights. It cannot, however, be denied, and
especially looking to the existing circumstances of Ragusa and Venice, that it was an

* See Appendini.

† Sir G. Wilkinson cites the examples of other Italian
Republics, who, to save themselves from the factious behaviour
of their ambitious citizens, also chose foreign governors. Thus
Verona, at the beginning of the thirteenth century, chose
Azzo, Marquis of Este. Florence, in 1303, was ruled by a
Lucchese, and in 1342 by the Duke of Athens. Similar
examples are to be found in the History of Sienna, Pisa,
Rimini, Ferrara, &c. It was Verona, according to Muratori,
which first set the example.

agreement calculated to give the latter great, nay, supreme influence in Ragusa; and accordingly there were not wanting those, especially amongst the Bobali, who deplored such a step, as being only the change of a domestic for a foreign master: one, which must with time succumb for want of means to sustain it, for another, which the power of Venice would render perpetual. But in vain; Pirro Benessa prevailed and went to Venice, where he was received by the senate, and his business favourably listened to. A treaty was made, in which the Venetians undertook the liberation of Ragusa on the sole stipulation of appointing one of their own citizens as count, which indeed Benessa thought a necessary safeguard against the divisions and jealousies of the Ragusan nobility. As regarded the execution of the treaty, this was to be effected after the usual fashion of the Venetians,—and scarcely less, it must be said, of most others in that age and nation,—by *stratagem.* Two galleys were placed at the disposal of Benessa, who was accompanied by the ambassadors and patriarch Morosini, then just on the point of sailing for Constantinople, and the captains of the vessels charged to pay implicit obedience to his orders. Having arrived under Lacroma, Benessa lost no time in going ashore to salute his father-in-law, and to urge him to receive the proffered visit of the distinguished Venetians, whom he pretended to be convoying to Constantinople; since, as he protested, they were moved to pay him so great a compliment only by their deep respect for his position and abilities. The unsuspicious Damian was not only drawn in to consent, but after entertaining them sumptuously, proceeded with fatal imprudence to return their visit on board. No sooner had he arrived and engaged in conversation than the anchor was weighed, and the astonished despot learnt, amidst the rattling of fetters, that his rule and liberty were both at an end. Though overreached, however, he was not subdued. Sternly accusing his son-in-law of parricide, and the Venetians of treachery, he dashed his head against the prow of the vessel, and fell down dead on the deck.* Such was the unfortunate end of Damian Judas, a man, as all agree, of great talent, and of consummate ability for governing. As to the nature of his designs, there was much dispute amongst his fellow citizens; the general feeling being apparently to regret him when it was too late. For they soon grew discontented with the rule of the Venetian counts, whom they regarded as seeking the interest of their own city at the expense of that which they were sent to govern : they accused them of doing every thing to irritate the Ragusans; of taking no pains to make them respected by the surrounding Slave nations, but rather the reverse, and of intriguing to render their own presidency perpetual. Yet, after an attempt

* A century later, the Venetian Proveditore, Andrea Dandolo, after losing the naval action at Curzola, and being taken prisoner by the Genoese, did exactly the same thing as Damian Judas, on the voyage to Genoa.

at the end of twenty-five years to do without, and struggling on alone for two years, they were again obliged to recall and submit to this method of administration during one hundred and fifty years, at the end of which, a fortunate combination of circumstances enabled them, with a good grace, to dispense with it. The Venetians, for some reason, voluntarily withdrew their count—not however without suspicion of ulterior designs— and the Ragusans, courteously thanking them for the good understanding which had so many years subsisted between them, proceeded at once to place themselves openly, as they had already done privately, under the protection of Louis the Great, King of Hungary.

Without pretending to decide upon the strict justice of each allegation brought by the Ragusans against their Venetian governors, still, calling to mind the ambitious character of that republic, and the overt acts of hostility and treachery of which it was convicted in its dealings with its smaller but still rival sister, we shall not perhaps feel disposed to doubt them as a whole. Yet, if we would be fair, we must also look on the other side of the picture, and pay attention to the advantages which, even on its own admission, Ragusa derived from its Venetian connexion.

First, as regards trade. It is obvious that one of the first, or, as we should rather say, *the* first of commercial cities of those days, was capable of bestowing great benefits both directly and indirectly on an inferior aspirant to that great source of national wealth and prosperity. The size and situation of Venice alone, considered relatively to the other European cities of those days, would make it a great market for Ragusan produce; besides which, it was so long established a mart, that *through* it their goods passed into a large part of Italy, and more distant countries beyond. The value of this is enhanced when we consider the scarcity of ports throughout the Italian peninsula, and especially on its eastern shore. The rocky coasts of Istria and Dalmatia teem with abundance of large and safe harbours formed by nature, in some of which, like that at Pola, a first-rate navy of modern days might ride without inconvenience. With the exception of Venice and Ancona, the opposite coast is destitute of anything which deserves the name; and of these, Ancona is unsafe, and Venice unsuited to modern navigation. But it was otherwise as regards the latter at the time we are speaking of. Then the safety of the intricate lagunes was appreciated, their shallowness but little felt, and the whole eastern trade passing up the gulf, Ragusa found there all the advantages of a great thoroughfare. Hence we can readily understand, that if, as we are assured by their historians, the first peace and commercial treaty with Venice, A.D. 1017, brought many advantages to the Ragusans, yet more would result from this present alliance, two centuries later, by virtue of which they were admitted to all the privileges of Venetian citizens.

But next, it also *civilized* them. Commerce with Italy had at all times the effect of bringing in a higher state of cultivation at Ragusa. The chief cities of that peninsula during the middle ages retained or revived much of its ancient intellectual pre-eminence in Europe. Ragusa, confined to a narrow strip of territory in the midst of semi-barbarous Slaves, was in this respect unfavourably situated. Hence, as long as they had any political existence, we find them striving to make up for their outlandish position by frequenting the polished courts and learned universities of Italy; such as, especially, those of Padua, of Florence, and of Sienna.

Neither was Venice less fitted to instruct them in the management of public affairs and all the details of political despatch, for her statesmen were amongst the most renowned in Europe for their skill in diplomacy. And all this, be it observed, without mentioning the important, though negative, advantage of escaping any worse intrigues against their liberty on the part of Venice, and passing unscathed through a century and a half, despite crisises at home or amongst their neighbours, which might have else proved fatal to all their hopes, without any one serious calamity. But the main advantage which they derived from the presence of the Venetian counts was due to the legal learning, the disinterested labours, and acknowledged impartiality of the Count Marco Giustiniani, whose honourable character is borne witness to by the Ragusans themselves in their observation, that, "though a Venetian, he rigorously observed the agreements between the Republics," and whose profound legal knowledge was attested by their constant use of his "Liber Statutorum" as the text-book of their lawyers ever after. This epoch, which gave Ragusa a regular code, was remarkable throughout Europe as a new era in legislation, especially in Italy, France, Switzerland, Spain, Germany, and England, the countries which have since become most distinguished for civilization and laws. In a word, when the Venetian counts came to Ragusa they found everything in disorder, no written code, no order in the offices, no safeguards to the constitution, but everything at the mercy of the officials for the time being, or the momentary will of their superiors and the supreme councils. *They* introduced the system of Venice, and so completely, that owing to this—assisted, perhaps, by the genius of the place, which, from similarity of origin and circumstances, naturally inclined to resemble the city of St. Mark's — Ragusa, in after years, obtained the name of " Venezia Minore."

Accordingly, with the fourteenth century, as the Venetian superintendence drew to a close, the climax of Ragusan prosperity commenced. Henceforth their commerce grew rapidly to its height. Abroad they had free access to all the ports of Venice; at home they excelled in all those arts which flourished there, *e.g.* dyeing, coining, making glass, shipbuilding, &c. Just at the end of this century, the Senate perceived that the time was come to reform their public schools; a task which they executed with success; and amongst other changes, introduced the study of the soft and poetical Illyrian dialect, which thus became known to the world of letters the earliest of all the Slave languages after the revival of learning * in the thirteenth and fourteenth centuries. A few years more, and their catalogue of writers commences. We shall not, therefore, be wrong in reckoning the temporary supremacy of the Venetians as a fortunate event for Ragusa, even while we regard its liberation from their interference, and the recovery of its former independence, as the causes of fresh vigour and a new impulse. So that while we acknowledge the latter as the immediate, we cannot deny that the former

---

* The revival of learning alluded to is that which took place coincident with the rise of the Italian Republics. See Sismondi. The University of Prague was founded in the middle of the fourteenth century: but neither Polish nor Bohemian became known in consequence beyond the borders of the nations which spoke them. › *Illyrian* was studied in Tuscany, for the sake of the Ragusan writers.

was, the remote cause of its success, whether commercial, political, or literary.

Hitherto we have considered Ragusa in its infancy and youth; we are now come to its zenith. The summary of its chronology is this: Possibly from the fifth, certainly from the seventh until the end of the thirteenth century, it was growing to its full proportions. During the fourteenth, fifteenth, and sixteenth, it flourished in the vigour of manhood. The seventeenth and eighteenth saw its old age and decrepitude. With the nascent nineteenth it sank into the grave.

But first, before proceeding farther in its history, we must examine briefly the character of its institutions at this, the period of its perfection. What the exact form of the constitution was before the arrival of the Venetians is subject to some doubt, owing to the failure of documents. Before the thirteenth century, written laws do not appear to have existed, and the rules upon which they acted were fixed by custom, and handed down by tradition. We can, however, judge of their general scope by remembering their origin under the Roman empire, and by considering what succeeded them without any appearance of radical alteration, which, besides, the Venetian counts, even had they been so minded, were little likely to have had the power of effecting, unpopular as they were. An important change, however, was introduced on the *departure* of the Venetians, in respect of the chief magistrate and his term of authority. This officer, chosen from the patricians and invested with limited powers, was originally entitled " Præses," prince, or president, and like the Gonfaloniero of Florence, &c., elected *annually*. Now, although his rank and dignity were maintained, his style was changed to that of " Rector;" his authority was more jealously and exactly determined, and his period of office expired at the end of a *month*.

The election to this highest post was in the hands of the great council of all the patricians, or " Togati," as they were called from their dress, but its powers were circumscribed, first by the Senate, or council of magistrates—a body of forty-five nobles, composed of all those who had held high offices in the state; secondly, by the " Consiglio Minore," which was formed of seven senators, who, with the rector, made up the executive; and thirdly, by three " Proveditori," who had the power of suspending laws, and were subordinate only to the Great Council and the Senate.

Society at large was divided into three classes,—patricians, citizens, and artisans. The latter were excluded from all share in government. The citizen, whose qualification consisted in a certain amount of real property, was eligible to the subordinate offices in the exchequer; the power of election being vested in the Senate. Every post of importance, with the sole exception of the admiral of the fleet, was filled by one of patrician birth; those of greater responsibility by the members of the Senate; those of lesser by the simple "Togati," to whom also, at large, as in ancient Rome, belonged the rights of patronage, the prosecution of suits and the advocacy of causes, and in whose great assembly, according to the theory of the constitution, the sovereign power was vested.

In a word, Ragusa was a pure aristocracy, with all the evils inseparable from that form of government, more especially where the ranks of the privileged orders are closed to all who do not chance to be born in them, and the merit which, hypothetically, once attained, that dignity becomes stereotyped to some former period in the recesses of ages gone by. It is evident that the natural tendency of such an order, as in Sparta, must be to come to an end, if only from the failure of numbers ; and it is highly probable that such would have been the fate of Ragusa long before the period of its dissolution—since we have it on record that within 600 years 222 noble and 300 civic families were quite obliterated—if it had not been for the practice, acted upon from the times of Paulimirus until the Turkish conquest,

T

of aggregating to the patrician and civic orders princes and nobles from the contiguous Slave provinces, and the neighbouring Italian towns, as often as the latter were compelled by political events, or other causes, to immigrate. For thus there was a constant fountain of supply, which, rising amongst their less cultivated and semi-barbarous neighbours, and flowing into the better-trained schools and more polished society of Ragusa, replenished the ranks of the upper classes, no less than the lower, with life and vigour. After the fall of the Slave dynasties, the invasion of the Turks, and the extension of the Venetian empire throughout maritime Dalmatia, these sources of supply were cut off, and the result of these conquests was, as we shall see, one of the causes which produced decay in the Ragusan commonwealth.

But such misfortunes, however fatal eventually, do not make themselves felt at once, neither was the exclusive merit of birth deemed so absurd an idea in the fourteenth and two following centuries as it came to be regarded in the eighteenth and nineteenth. That a certain lineage should be considered the only road to the highest honours which the state has to confer, presented no insuperable difficulty to European theorists of those times. Rather the contrary; with the writers of that date it is just that which they find to praise. "This republic, of all which we have found," says Bodin,* "preserves an aristocracy the purest and farthest removed from the interference of the people." In the words of Lipsius,† it was "the noble republic which divided civilization from barbarism, in laws and manners highly polished:" and with Sabellicus,‡ "the free state most excellently provided with laws and institutions." And no doubt they were not so unsuited to the dispositions of men's minds in those times. They roused the noble and citizen to exertion,

* Jean Bodin, a French writer, flourished A.D. 1570.
† Justus Lipsius, a Dutchman, flourished A.D. 1590.
‡ Sabellicus, an Italian, flourished A.D. 1480-90.

while the peasant and artisan but little felt their own exclusion. The poor, indeed, it must be owned, are practically much alike in all ages. Compelled by the stern law of necessity to work at their respective callings for their daily supply of food and raiment, they have little time or inclination to trouble themselves with the aspirations which occupy others better provided with this world's goods. Every settled government, in which the rights of property are respected, is, in this point of view, more or less of an aristocracy. The difference between those more remote times and our own lies chiefly in this, that *then* honours were as much as possible open to birth only; now they are made, in theory, at least, accessible to every one who *has means and genius*. Stimulated, then, not depressed, by their aristocratic form of government, the patricians and citizens of Ragusa emulated one another in commercial enterprise and in the path of letters. As was natural, their commerce and material wealth grew to its climax first: as the commoner and more hardy plant, it also lasted longest.

We have seen that it was " a duris urgens in rebus egestas " that the Ragusans first turned to the sea for support. It is indeed probable that Epidaurus and Salonæ owed their beginnings to that broad bosom, which in all ages has formed the high road of commercial enterprise. Epidaurus, founded by the trading Greeks, stood on a peninsula united to the mainland by a narrow isthmus. Salonæ, which from its Cyclopean remains must date from a yet remoter antiquity, is placed above the banks of a river, near its estuary—a situation well suited to the piratical habits and experience of the earliest navigators. But when the site of Ragusa was chosen, it was not a question of mercantile convenience, but, as we have seen, of security against barbarian neighbours, and of obtaining the necessaries of life. Had they been what they became in after years, they would have surely preferred the vicinity of the commodious harbour of Gravosa, or raised habitations on the foundations still existing at Alt-Ragusa, instead of the stony and, as the disastrous result proved, volcanic Dubrownik. Still, notwithstanding the inconveniences of the spot, with time they overcame all impediments.

From the first, their marine grew apace. In the ninth century they could undertake the transport of Slave-troops to Italy; towards the latter part of the tenth, the Venetians captured successively two of their merchantmen, afterwards reclaimed, whose cargoes were valued at fifty thousand ducats, or more than £11,000 sterling. About the same time they joined the fleet of the Narentans and Greeks going to make war on Venice. Some of their ships were with Robert Guiscard, the Norman, when he defeated Alexis Comnenus and the doge Domenico Sylvio, near Durazzo. Others they sent with each crusade. But it was in the fourteenth century that their maritime commerce made the most rapid strides. As will appear, also, on other occasions it was wont to alternate with their inland trade, which, at this moment, while Venice was admitting them to great advantages to sea-wards, received a severe check in the confusion which followed the extinction of the Nemagna dynasty, and the consequent abolition of their former privileges. About the middle of this century (A. D. 1338), the power of Louis of Hungary protected them against the intrigues of Venice; and again, twenty years later, the formidable Genoese league, to which the Ragusans adhered, and by means of which they established permanent relations with Genoa, shortly to be extended to France also. Urban V. now gave them a special permission to traffic with infidels, which grew daily more imperative from the progress of the Mussulman arms. On the strength of this permission, which was confirmed at the council of Bâsle in the following century, not only did they enter into commercial relations with the governments of Syria and Egypt and the islands of the Archipelago, but in A.D. 1370 they sent an embassy with a present of foreign fruit to Orcan, the Grand Signior of the Turks, who, invited into Europe by the usurper of Bulgaria, had marched victorious throughout the Greek empire. The conqueror, complimented by this tribute to the fame of his arms, concluded a favourable treaty with the remote little commonwealth, accepted a tribute of about £200 sterling, and in return, "set his hand to the deed" in a way highly characteristic of that barbarous ignorance which is still the prevailing feature of his nation, viz. by dipping his hand in the ink and applying it to the paper. The original document was long [*] preserved at Ragusa, and, like some sacred relic, still excited the admiration and reverence of Mussulman spectators.

The climax of their maritime prosperity was in the fifteenth and early sixteenth centuries. There was then, according to

* That is, till the beginning of this century.
† Palladio Fosco, ap. Appendini.

the testimony of a contemporary writer,
" no part of Europe so concealed, so hostile
to strangers, that you did not find there
the Ragusan merchant." On the other hand
every nation found shelter in their harbours,
not excepting those who were at war with the
Ottoman Porte, for even the Turk was compelled to respect Ragusa's neutrality. Especially the Venetians, during the league, so disastrous for them, of Cambrai, flocked there whilst
shut out everywhere else. So long as the Cape
of Good Hope remained undiscovered, they had
the Indian trade across Egypt, and afterwards
they did but turn their enterprise more towards
the western shores of Europe, where they had
a great commerce with Spain and not a little
with England and Holland. Even more than
a century later, when they were beginning to
decline, Cromwell, in an extant letter to their
Senate, granted them special privileges in all the
British seas. But their chief intercourse was
with Spain, for whose government under Ferdinand and Isabella they engaged to transport

back the Moors to the coast of Africa. Hence arose a great friendship, which, however profitable at first, resulted eventually in the ruin of the Ragusan navy, the whole of which perished in the fatal wars of the Spanish monarchs, as we shall presently see. This however did not take place until the reputation of Ragusan merchantmen for wealthy cargoes had been stereotyped in the word Argosy (quasi Ragosy)— synonymous for the richest kind of carack.

But it was their *land* trade which *first* brought them fortune and distinction. This commenced about the ninth century, when they agreed to pay a small sum to each ban for permission to traffic in his dominions. They made it a monopoly, more especially with respect to the gold and silver from the rivers and mines of Bosnia. Not much is known of this source for obtaining the precious metals, which was quite lost after the arrival of the Turks. So much appears certain, that the Ragusans worked mines for silver, that in the same neighbourhood gold* sand was found in considerable abundance, and that the silver called "glava" came into commerce mixed with gold.†

* Pliny says, that under the Emperor Nero, the province of Dalmatia produced 50 lbs. weight of gold daily. It was found " in summo cespite," " on the surface of the ground," that is, probably, in the sand of the beds of the rivers.—Plin. Hist. Nat. lib. xxxiii. 4. Florus tells us, that Vibius, who was left by Augustus to subdue the Dalmatians, made them "work mines and purify gold ;" and Martial calls Dalmatia, *i. e.* about Salona, " aurifera."

> " Ibis litoreas, Macer, Salonas ; . . .
> Felix auriferæ colone terræ."—Epig. x. 78.

Statius speaks of Dalmatia as proverbial,—like Peru or California—

> "Robora Dalmatico lucent satiata metallo."
> STATIUS, *in Epithalamio Stellæ.*

But the Abate Fortis at the end of the last century found no mines in Dalmatia, except one of iron. See his Viaggio, in Dalmazia, Kerke, § 8, vol. i. p. 128. Probably he did not examine beyond the coast, the hills of which, he adds, "look unlikely for mines, which if they exist must be *in the interior.*" Even now the Zingari, or gipsies, are said to make a trade of gold sand, which they collect on the banks of the rivers of Bosnia. The ornaments, too, of coins and tinsel, which one still sees in the hair and on the dress of the Slave women on the Austrian military frontiers, originated in this way. The Ragusans made immense profits by their share in the business, whencesoever it reached them.

† A gift of Queen Margaret, of Bosnia, consisting of 200 lbs. of silver, contained also gold in the proportion of 2 oz. to the pound.

The trade with Slavonia once established was constantly on the increase, notwithstanding the interruptions which ensued from the frequent domestic wars of its princes; an ever-recurring evil which they were obliged to meet by claiming the protection of the bans against the kings, and again of the latter against the bans and grandees. Especially their influence grew through the asylums which the commonwealth opened to all the unfortunate princes, and the fidelity with which it defended their causes. Thus in process of time they pushed their colonies far beyond Slavonia and its quarrelsome chieftains, nay, into every province of the ancient Byzantine empire, e.g. Belgrad, Rusich, Silistria, Adrianople, and Sophia— which was the chief of them—and finally under the later Greek emperors extended them even into Mysia and the rest of Asia Minor. Their further progress was checked by the invasion of the Turks, and the new direction which commerce now began to take.

Still the existing establishments continued, to the comfort of resident Catholics and of all European travellers, keeping up a trade with the Turks in skins, wax, wool, silk and damask. So that even as late as after the calamities occasioned by the Spanish wars and the great earthquake, their merchants were enabled by means of this land trade, which then alone remained to them of all their former sources of wealth, to rebuild their ships, and, on a small scale, re-establish their marine. Besides these resources abroad, they had divers home manufactures. At the end of the fifteenth century, a Florentine nobleman established a cloth manufactory. In the sixteenth, one of their own brought in the art of weaving silk stuffs. They made salt in abundance on the promontory of Sabbioncello,—or Punta, as it is also called,— and indeed everything generally which was produced at Venice came within their scope. They cast ordnance, exported dyes, and oil for the long fasts of the Greeks, and fished up coral, for which great search was made in those days throughout the Mediterranean. Their merchants enjoyed the wealth of petty princes. Mattia Luccari, not the richest of them we are assured, was able to receive and conceal in his house at Rascia, king, later emperor, Sigismund after his defeat by the Turks, and further to present him with 15,000 zechins, or nearly 7,000*l*. sterling, besides other gifts. Another left 200,000 zechins to the republic. Tradition says that the merchants of one quarter of their little city possessed a capital of between four and five million pounds. Latterly, besides paying a heavy tribute, more than £3,000,* to the sultan for free commerce, remunerating with handsome salaries all their own officers of state and foreign ministers, keeping in good repair their numerous public buildings at home and abroad, pensioning the exiled princes, their guests, sustaining numerous converts from Islamism and the Greek schism, and other like acts of liberality, they incurred over and above

---

* Sandys calls it 14,000 sequins, at the date of his travels, *i. e.* middle of the seventeenth century.

a vast and increasing outlay to keep off the plague, which so early as before the year A.D. 1400 had amounted to more than three million sterling,—expenses which a revenue of £36,000 yearly from customs alone enabled this " gate of the East" to accomplish.

The literature of Ragusa was of tardier growth. "Sapientia scribæ in tempore vacuitatis." Leisure is the first condition of learning, and leisure depends upon wealth and peace. The literature of Ragusa, therefore, naturally dates from the fifteenth century, when the commonwealth, civilized by connexion with Venice, enriched by an extensive commerce, and secured by the power of their patrons, the kings of Hungary, had time to regulate its public schools, and cultivate the Muses. Coincident with that epoch, occurred an event, which, spreading its influence over all European cities, reached Ragusa amongst the very first. This was the fall of Constantinople before the arms of Mahomet II., the dispersion of its men of letters, and the consequent revival of classical taste in art and literature throughout the civilized world. The little republic was one of the first to profit by it. Latin, once the language of its population, had never entirely ceased to be spoken there, though widely differing in later ages from the Augustan standard. But now, an appreciation of the latter reviving in Europe, the Senate lost no time in inviting Filippo de Diversis de Quartigianis from Lucca, to give instructions therein, and afterwards the more distinguished Demetrius Calcondila, who taught Latin and Greek, at a salary of five hundred crowns per annum. Besides these, many other illustrious scholars were prevailed on to stop at Ragusa, as they passed along the Adriatic on their road to Venice and Lombardy, to Tuscany and Rome. In fact, during the fifteenth and sixteenth centuries, learning had made such progress, that every noble and wealthy family could boast of their *literati* amongst its members. And of these not a few bore a European reputation. Such were Elio Lampridio Cervino, crowned at Rome—as Milton was 150 years later at Florence—for his Latin verses, under Sixtus IV.; Marino Ghetaldi, born 1566 of a noble and distinguished family, originally of Tarentum—which is said to have been founded at the same time, and by the same colonists as Ragusa—who travelled through Germany, France, Italy, and England, where he resided for two years, and on account of the purity of his manners, and his profound knowledge of mathematics, obtained the honourable *soubriquet* of "Angelo di costumi e demonio in Matematica;" and of whom Appendini does not hesitate to assert, that he might have been a Newton, had he lived when knowledge was more advanced: Stefano Gradi, librarian to the Vatican under Urban VIII. and Alexander VII.; and last, but by no means least, the Jesuit, Roger Joseph Boscovich, in the last century (he was born 1711, and died 1781), whose " new system of natural philosophy alone will render his name

immortal;" and who, to say nothing of his
skill in writing Latin poetry, must ever rank
amongst the first of European mathematicians
and philosophers.

But it is for its Slave poets that Ragusa
is justly celebrated,—poets who could scarcely
have failed to rival Tasso and Metastasio in
public estimation, were the language in which
they wrote equally easy of access with the
Italian.   But of all the great European languages, the most widely extended is also the
most difficult of attainment, and for this,
as well as other causes, the least studied;
undeservedly, if we regard the capabilities of
that language, its flexibility, its richness, its
power of expressing the soft, the tender, the
melancholy, and scarcely less every other
passion of the human heart, its numerous
forms of verbs, calculated to describe every
variety of action, its accurate inflexions, which,
like the Latin, dispense with the article, and
admit of an harmonious and happy transpo-
sition of words, quite beyond the powers of

every other European language; undeservedly so far, but not undeservedly, perhaps,—at least quite intelligibly,—if, in connexion with its difficulty, we regard the poverty of its literature, and, in a word, the judgment of the Slaves themselves, who, patiently submitting to the supremacy of every foreign tongue, have preferred, until quite recent times at least, to use the languages of other nations, German or Italian, or French, to their own melodious but uncultivated dialects.

The first scholars who wrote poetry in Slave were Ragusans. The Russian, the Polish, the Bohemian authors, except for ancient bardic compositions, about on a par with Ossian and the Niebelungen Noth, are posterior to the Darsich, Menzi, Vetrani, nay more, to the Gondolas and Palmottas of the republic. It would, indeed, be difficult in any race of Slave descent to find an epoch when they were without poetry in proportion to their advancement, and, therefore, in saying so

much, we are only claiming an earlier cultivation for the Ragusan writers, which they
gained through their connexion with Italy,
than other branches of their race enjoyed.
There is no doubt there were Slave *poets*
at Ragusa five centuries before the earliest
of the writers named above. Zuccari,* a
native historian, mentions how one of the
Narentan princes, in the tenth century, was
induced to protect the Ragusans by their
ballads, which celebrated the deeds of his
countrymen. Another† records the "popievka"
or "lay" which was composed on the shipwreck of Alexius Comnenus in the Gulph
of Lyons, circa A.D. 1100. Their "shenitne,"
and "kolendiske piesme," or "nuptial songs,"
and "Christmas carols," are of remote antiquity, and exist among the Austrian Wends
to this day no less than amongst the Dalmatian Slaves.

---

* Giacomo Zuccari was both a considerable traveller and
a man of learning. His history of Ragusa was published at
Venice, A.D. 1605.

† Benedict Caboga, died A.D. 1590.

It is of such "popievke," or national ballads,* that what is termed the first epoch of their poetry consists. But the study of Illyrian being introduced into the schools (about A.D. 1400), a new era commenced in which Menzi and Darsich, two of the first who *wrote* their verses, represent, according to the talented Abate Giorgi, their Petrarch and Boccaccio. From these there was a regular and steady advance to the Dervish of Gozze,† the Zingara, or gipsy of Cjubranovich, and the odes of Ragnina and Slatarich, who, being well read in the best authors of Greece and Rome,

* They have been collected and printed by Vuk Stefano-vich, under the title of Crbske Narodne Piesme, Leipsig, 1825. A selection of them was translated into English, and published by Sir John Bowring.

† Gozze was a patrician Being confined for some political offence in the Rectorial House, he had suffered his beard to grow, in order to express his melancholy condition. In this state, as he was walking in the central court of the palace for exercise, he attracted the attention of the Rector's daughter, who, mistaking him for some Oriental, asked, "Chi è questo Dervish?" On these words he wrote his poem, called the Dervishiata, in prison. Subsequently he obtained both his liberty and the hand of the lady. A very similar story is told of the origin of the Zingara.

and more modern Italy, presented their countrymen with copious versions of great beauty from each of these languages, and introduced every style and metre into their native tongue. Such was the progress of poetry in Ragusa, when (circa 1610) Giovanni Gondola, that bright ornament of Slave poets, brought it to its zenith. A somewhat longer notice of the author of the Osmanid and his works may not be without its interest. He was born A.D. 1588, of an illustrious and patrician family; his father, Francis, being in the senate, and having formerly borne the dignity of the republic's minister at Constantinople, a post which at that time expressed nothing short of readiness to sacrifice life for country. Giovanni inherited the virtues and piety of his father. IIis early works were all composed on religious subjects, e.g. "A metrical Version of the Penitential Psalms," "The Tears of the Prodigal Son," "The Mysteries of Religion," &c.; and it is further related of him, that, in accordance with such a tone of mind, he used to pass the Holy Week in spiritual exercises on the rock of Daxa, amongst the religious of the order of St. Francis. Afterwards he brought out some dramas, *e.g.* "Ariadne," "The Rape of Proserpine," and a translation of the Gerusalemme Liberata, all of which perished in the earthquake. When exactly the Osmanid was published is uncertain; but the historical events on which it is based occurred in 1621, and the poet died 1638. The principal subject of this masterpiece of Illyrian poetry is "the fate of Osman;" that Sultan, who in 1621 invaded the kingdom of Poland, was defeated by Prince Vladislav, the son of King Sigismund, and compelled to make peace. Attributing the discomfiture of his army to the decay of ancient discipline, and attempting extensive reforms, he was dethroned and killed in the revolution which followed. It would not be possible, within the limits of this sketch, to give any adequate idea of the Osmanid, a poem which extends through twenty-two cantos, of several hundred lines each. But briefly it may be stated to be written in the heroic style of the "Gerusalemme," of which, as already observed, its author had been the Illyrian translator. Thus, while the main interest centres round Osman, the young sultan, his aspirations and his misfortunes, a variety of episodes are introduced, analogous to those in the "Gerusalemme," which add much to its beauty as a whole, and relieve the sombre colouring which a foresight of the tragic but historical *dénouement* naturally casts over it. As might be expected from an author deeply versed in the best models of the classical languages of antiquity, and of the Italian revival, and in the sacred Scriptures, its composition is of the highest order, the versification excellent, the language, with some few grammatical drawbacks, correct, and the descriptions graphic yet dignified. But above all there is a brilliancy in the imagery, a warmth and

pathos in the passions, an elevation of senti-
ment, and an originality of ideas, which
stamp it as a *chef d'œuvre*, and give Gondola a claim to be classed with, nay even
before, Torquato Tasso.

A relation of Gondola of the same date,
and only a degree less distinguished, was
Giugno Palmotta, whose "Christiad," or
"Life of Christ," in twenty-four cantos, is
also a work of wonderful beauty, piety, and
elegance; one might add simplicity and
originality; for it is the simple narrative
from the four Gospels, ornamented with
poetic lights and shades, and only here and
there filled out from ancient traditional
sources. The mode of treating and working the respective parts in detail is also
original. Yet the idea of it, as a whole,
was taken from a Latin poem on the same
subject published in Italy about a century
earlier by Jerome Vida.* This composition,
inferior in all respects to his own, he took

---

* Jerome Vida, Bishop of Alba, flor. A.D. 1540.

as his model, aiming, we are assured, much more at inculcating his thesis, as the most profitable subject-matter for meditation on the minds of the Ragusan youth, than at obtaining the fame of genius or even originality, which he yet merited. His powers of rapid composition were astonishing, and might be well compared with those of Lope de Vegas, and others of the Spanish school, whom he resembled too in purity of ideas, and a deep serene devotion.

The last of the Ragusco-Illyrian poets was Ignazio Giorgi (mentioned above), who flourished in the seventeenth and beginning of the eighteenth centuries, after the great earthquake. He was distinguished not only for the excellence of his poetry in each of the three languages in vogue at Ragusa—Latin, Italian, and Illyrian—but also as an antiquary, in which capacity his view of "St. Paul's Shipwreck on Meleda," off the coast of Dalmatia near Ragusa, "not Malta," is well known,—an opinion which, however little weight we may attach to it now, he supported with such eloquence and vigour, as to convince some scholars, as *e. g.* Facciolati, and more recently our own countryman, Bryant. As a poet, his Illyrian compositions were principally esteemed, and of these the most famed is his "Usdari Mandaljene," or "Tears of the Penitent Magdalen." This poem, unlike the foregoing, is written in stanzas of six instead of four lines, is more elaborate, not inferior in imagination or versification, and contains many proofs of the varied scholarship of its author. Still it wants the simplicity of Palmotta, and the dignity of Gondola; it flags in interest, betrays a tendency to mannerism, and, in a word, marks the decadence of Illyrian poetry at Ragusa, where it never rose again. In short, as Gondola was the Raphael, so Giorgi was the Carlo Dolci of his art and country.

While we are speaking of the mental cultivation attained to by Ragusan society, it must not be forgotten that the fair sex also were distinguished not only by the general refinement of their manners and their devotion to the education of their children, but also by proficiency in the severer studies and as authoresses, of whom, during the three centuries that literature flourished there, nearly a dozen names are recorded. This fact is not the less remarkable when we remember that twelve was the ordinary age for marriage.

One of the most celebrated of these was Floria Zuzzeri, born 1555, and married, according to the prevailing custom, in 1567, to Bartolomeo Pescioni, a gentleman of Florence, where, passing the half of each year with her husband, she was no less famed than at Ragusa. Her epigrams, written in Slave and Italian (though the havoc occasioned by the frequent fires and earthquakes of her native soil has not suffered them to come down to us), bore high repute in their day for clearness and refinement of thought as well as elegance of style. It was to her that Ragnina and Slatarich and Gozze, and his wife Maria Gondola, the authoress of a treatise on the

Meteors of Aristotle, dedicated their works. The same compliment she received from Marino Battilore in his "Rime Toscane di Monaldi." Unfortunately she died young (about A.D. 1600).

We have her portrait, which appearing occasionally in our exhibitions proves that she was with justice no less renowned for personal attractions than for poetical merit.

We have already mentioned the custom which prevailed during those centuries of sending their youth to graduate in the universities of Italy, to Padua and Pavia, to Pisa and Sienna, and to frequent such courts as that of Florence, which was then, in the sixteenth century, flourishing as the resort of the learned and scientific under the Medicis. The *literati* of Ragusa met with flattering attentions from those princes. Domenico Ragnina was made chevalier of St. Stephen by the great Cosmo I., a few years after that Prince had established this famous military order as a reward for distinguished merit (A. D. 1560).

Cosmo III. himself studied Illyrian, retaining as his preceptor, during three years, Marino Gondola, a relation of the poet, at his court, that he might master the difficulties of the Osmanid. The same prince made Anselmo Banduri, the Ragusan antiquarian, his secret minister at the court of Louis XIV., and the regent Duke of Orleans, which eventually led to Anselmo's becoming librarian to the latter, in which post he died, 1743.

While these distinguished themselves in Tuscany and France, Domenico Slatarich rendered himself no less conspicuous for another class of abilities during the latter part of the sixteenth century at Venice and Padua. We have already had occasion to mention him as belonging to the chain of Illyrian poets. We must now relate his able conduct during his residence at the university of Padua, where he was elected " Gymnasiarch," or " Rector of the Students, with authority also over the Professors," by the university. This office, which was abolished during the next century, when the numbers of the students began to fall off, was, at the time of which we are speaking, of high dignity, giving rank next to the bishop and governor of the place: hence it was usually filled by a patrician of character, wealth, and ability. Now it happened that whilst he held it, there arose a very dangerous disturbance amongst the young men, who amounted, inclusive of foreigners, to seven thousand. This began in a quarrel between the French and German students, but soon spreading amongst the rest, who took part with one side or the other, became general. At last it came to blows; Frederic Corner, the bishop, having in vain attempted to interpose, and an officer sent by the governor being killed in the affray, the belligerents marched out of the town with drums and bells, and encamped without the gates. It was at this critical juncture that Slatarich interposed, and, acting with the podestà, had the dexterity to persuade both sides to lay down their arms and return to good order, to the great satisfaction of the Venetian Senate, who in reward created him " Cavaliere aurato," a distinction which was at that period still confined to real merit.

Ragusa was, therefore, scarcely less renowned in the literary than in the commercial world.

We have yet something to say on its steady zeal for religion and undeviating adherence to the Church, which were in fact its most honourable title to the respect of the rest of Christendom, and especially to its almost uninterrupted friendship with the popes. Incidentally this has not been altogether overlooked, but a point of so much importance merits a separate mention, and we will therefore here, as briefly as possible, collect together in one point of view those scattered notices; adding, at the same time, how it escaped the troubles of the sixteenth century, which convulsed and agonised so many other cities, with a few remarks on some of its customs and usages, especially respecting the education and conduct of youth, whence we may form an idea of its peculiar genius and moral character.

Even in the days of its infancy, we found Ragusa fighting in the ranks of the Church. Thus it was when the Saracens encamped on Gargano and fortified Bari. Thus it was again when the common enemies of Christianity were to be dispossessed of the occupation of those sacred places, which religion renders dear to every Christian heart. Thus it was, in another sense, but not less truly, when the Slaves began to fall off from the unity of the Church, and their princes, especially the treacherous line of Nemagna, to be Catholic or Greek by profession, just as it suited some base end. For then Ragusa formed a rallying point to the Catholics, and provided the Popes with a safe cathedra, whence they could exhort them to return to the fold, wherein they had received the rudiments of faith and civilization. Their colonies protected Catholics amongst schismatic Greeks, civilized men amongst

x

barbarians, Christians amongst Turks. Their
religious, over and above the parochial clergy,
comprehending four orders, viz. Benedictines,
Franciscans, Dominicans, and Jesuits, counted
eighteen different establishments for men and
eight for women, liberally endowed and distinguished for learning. Their Benedictines alone
possessed five abbeys, and produced a succession of authors, of whom, besides lesser names,
Cervario, Caboga, Vetrani, Orbini, in early, and
Giorgi in later times, have all left valuable,
chiefly historical, monuments of their literary
labours. That the Franciscan library was one
of the finest in that order, appears from the scale
of that of the restoration, made with greatly
diminished resources, and, indeed, in every
respect immeasurably inferior to that which
preceded it. Two bishoprics, of Trebigne and
Stagno, owed their foundation to the zeal of
the republic. To their credit is to be reckoned
the support of Christians, who had fled from
the fury of the Mussulman;—of converts who
had escaped from Islamism and schism;—of

priests, churches, and walled burial-grounds *
throughout the dominions of the Ottoman
Porte, wherever, that is, their colonies extended;
—to their honour was entrusted the safe conduct of travellers in those parts, their preservation in dangers, their assistance [in troubles,
and, in a word, such advantages to Christians
generally, that not. only Catholics, but all
Europeans who had occasion to risk themselves in those countries, were glad to pass as
Ragusans.

One only amongst the authors of Ragusa
was attracted by the doctrines of the Reformation. Matthias Flaccus, surnamed the
Illyrian, an historian, and a man of ability,
who had been educated at Venice, embraced
Lutheranism. He retired into Germany, and
became one of the centuriators of Magde-
burgh. Thence attempting to get his book
surreptitiously introduced and circulated in

* Walled burial-grounds were granted by special privilege
to the Ragusans, from the very first, out of respect for their
treaty with Orcan, before even a Christian chapel was allowed
to the French ambassador.

Ragusa, it was suppressed, and publicly burnt by order of the Senate. The author died in 1575, and this appears to have been the only attempt worth mentioning to propagate the Reformation at Ragusa.

When we spoke, in the beginning, of their preserving friendly relations with the rest of Europe, notwithstanding their commercial treaties and alliances with the Turks, there is no doubt that they were greatly assisted by the systematic neutrality they preserved, their respectability as merchants, the smallness of their narrow territory, its impotence for aggression, and its convenience as the door of trade to Slavonia first, and afterwards to Turkey. But it is also no less true that they never gave the Christian powers any just cause of offence by neglecting their duties as a Christian state, except in so far as it could be reckoned blameworthy that they adhered steadfastly to their policy of non-interference in the wars with the Turks, which, they might fairly argue, was the unavoidable consequence of their peculiar geographical position, and the necessary condition of their utility to Europe. Hence, their most constant friends were the popes. Pius II., IV., V., and Clement IX. they counted amongst their greatest benefactors. Pius V. it was, of glorious memory, who first dignified their state —hitherto styled Città, Civita, or Comune— with the name of " Republic." Clement IX. recalled them, phœnix-like, from their ashes. In all their misfortunes, whether threatened by the Turks or menaced by domineering Christian powers, Rome was their constant friend and resource, but above all, as we shall see, in the great and crowning calamity of the seventeenth century.

The manners and customs of the republic have been celebrated for their characteristic peculiarities. To enter into them in detail here would be beside the scope of these pages; but even a slight attention to the rise, growth, and a situation of the state will reveal the source of most of them. An Italian town deriving its origin from classic times, a Slave population amalgamated with the Italian element which pre-existed, a civilization matured under Venetian superintendence, the whole closely hemmed in by an Oriental government and the Mahometan religion, which, by the republic's own desire, lest their territory should be exposed to the dangerous contiguity of the Lion of St. Mark's, insulated them.

Such were the circumstances of Ragusa. The Slaves are everywhere remarkable for the number of their national customs, the tenacity with which they adhere to them, and the similarity which pervades them in countries disunited by great distances. Hence, then, a large proportion of those usages which impressed the spectator in Ragusa, *e.g.* the "kolende," or carols sung at certain festivals; the fires lighted outside the houses at night-fall on St. John Baptist's eve, over which the bystanders, crowned with garlands, leapt, crying "Evviva!" to the saint; the blessed

paschal bread; * the sending of cakes, as
"kolatz," *i.e.* a great circle or ring of bread,
"pogatcha," made of fine flour and almonds,
still sold in Venice under the name of "pane
Schiavone," &c., as presents on solemn occasions; of hiring "plakavitze," or women,
whose office it is to lament the dead with
loud and peculiar cries, accompanied with
beating of the breast and tearing of the hair;
these and numerous others have a *Slave*
origin. *Classical* was the panegyric pronounced in Latin over the corpse of a person
of distinction; † the taking the impression of
the face in wax, and carrying it in solemn
procession through the city; ‡ and the
habitual use of the "toga" by the nobles.
One custom appears as if it might have
descended from their remote Greek ancestors,
a remnant of the festival called "Dendro-

* These customs exist no less in Carniola, and all the
countries of the Wends.
† A nobleman, secretary, chancellor, or state physician.
‡ This was confined to the rector, archbishop, and head-
secretary.

phoria." At Easter, the patrician youth
formed themselves into a "druschina," or
confraternity, and dividing themselves, under
leaders, into two companies, brought a large
green branch into the town, which they
planted in front of the church of St. Blaise,
their patron saint. The two parties then contended for the possession of the tree, with
discharges of fireworks, and finally burnt it
amidst a grand display of the same on the
evening of the 3d of May, the "feast of Holy
Cross."

But other features—like a portion of their
vegetation, the palms, the aloes, the pomegranates—bore witness to Ragusa's southern
position and Mussulman neighbours. Of
such was the national dress, not differing
materially from Turk or Greek—the famous
red slippers or "paputche," the bag breeches,
the tasseled skull-cap, the "hangjar," or long
knife, and pistols exposed to view: of such
the Turkish bazaar or caravanna: of such that
young women, after the age of twelve years,

—when they ordinarily married, however—
went no more into the society of the opposite
sex, except in the care of fathers and brothers
and their nearest of kin; that if they must
go abroad, they chose the most retired
routes; that in church they occupied places
apart from observation; that the ladies generally went out in sedan-chairs, attended by
maid-servants habited " en capucines; " * that
young men could not ask in marriage for
themselves, because to suffer a refusal would
have been highly indecorous in the eyes of
society; they were expected to await the
advances of fathers or guardians who had
daughters or wards to marry. Praiseworthy,
whencesoever they had it, was the hospitality
of their upper classes, the frank, good-hearted
joviality of the lower, the simplicity of all.
They prided themselves on the bringing-up of
their children, and the pure Italian which
they taught them. Thus, we are told that
parents looked themselves to the task of
education—a satisfactory proof of intellectual

* *i. e.* a brown-coloured dress.

and moral culture in the parent, and a happy
omen for the future member of society; that
the presence of one elder preserved strict
order and decorum amongst the young; that,
besides this Spartan virtue, they also enjoined
great simplicity of diet; that for recreations,
those in vogue were chiefly field-sports, or,
if they indulged in theatricals, it was in
dramas, written by themselves in their native
Illyrian, of pure morality and lofty sentiments,
the representation of which they also took
upon themselves, to the exclusion of foreign
actors and actresses.

Thus the commonwealth flourished in reputation for religion and morals, as well as
literature and trade; and Watkins, an English
traveller in the eighteenth century, whom Sir
G. Wilkinson calls an unbiassed authority,
gives a very favourable picture of their character. He praises all classes, but especially
the nobles and upper ranks of citizens, who
as a rule, he avers, have all the good qualities
which a good example and a refined education are calculated to inspire, without the

vices of countries more exposed to foreign commerce, and therefore more versed in the arts of deception. "They have more learning," says he, "and less ostentation, more politeness and less envy, more hospitality to strangers, and in a word fewer defects than in any people, who have come within the range of my experience, so that I do not hesitate to pronounce Ragusa the wisest, the best, and the happiest of states."

But the republic of Ragusa, like all other human institutions, was destined to come to an end, and accordingly it had within it, probably from its first foundation, the seeds of its decay. An important item amongst these, viz. the exclusiveness of its upper classes, civic as well as noble, has been already touched upon. To this we shall have occasion to refer once more. In the meanwhile there are three causes strongly predisposing to their final ruin, which demand our attention, and the consideration of which will bring us far towards the end of their

history. The first of these are the conse-
quences of the Turkish invasion.

From the departure of the Venetian counts
to the final establishment of the Osmanlis
in Constantinople and the neighbourhood of
Ragusa, a century elapsed. During this
period the Ragusans were rising rapidly in
commercial prosperity, and laying the foundations of their future literary renown; while
their territory, enlarged by purchase and gift
from the lands of the bordering Slave princes,
attained its greatest extent.*

This was indeed a period of glory for the
little republic, which maintained its independence notwithstanding the mighty strife
raging around, sustained by the vast strength
of the Ottoman on the one side, and the
political genius of Venice on the other. In
the meanwhile the affairs of Slavonia grew

* This was a narrow strip from seventy to eighty miles in
extent along the coast, including the Promontory (or Punta)
of Hyllus (or Sabioncello), varying in breadth, but never
exceeding a few miles. Then the islands Meleda and Lagosta;
with the three Elaphites, i. e. Calamoto, di Mezzo and
Giupana; and the island of Lacroma.

every day more and more critical. Its unhappy rulers, divided by their separate territories, differing from one another in religion, and continually weakening the whole body by their intestine feuds, pulled down their houses, as it were, with their own hands, and during the last twenty years, when the danger had grown imminent, instead of uniting for the common defence, invited their own destruction by calling in on every occasion the crafty and all too powerful Turk, who lay at hand expecting his opportunity to seize and devour them.

Ragusa had already once given umbrage to the Osmanlis, and even hung some while suspended between the wrath and admiration of Amurath, because she befriended with an asylum, according to her ancient practice, and steadily refused to surrender up George, despot of Servia, who had fled thither with his family. At length the great crash came. Constantinople fell; all the provinces of the ancient Eastern empire were in a moment overrun, and the conqueror of Constantinople, Thrace, Servia, Bosnia, and great part of Hungary, had actually mounted his horse to carry his victorious arms through the maritime Dalmatia also, and he destined Ragusa, in vain calling on the sovereigns of Christendom for their promised succours, to be his special prey. The city was already filled with the fugitive voivods and nobles of Herzegovina, with their wives and children, who had fled thither as a last resource. Already they regarded themselves as lost. Already they seemed destitute of all human aid, and the whole population was giving itself to fasting, alms-giving, and prayer, when suddenly the report spreads that Mahomet, who was already in the adjoining province, is advancing! Then the horror and desolation of the city rose to its height, and it may be conceived with what solemnity the whole population came forth from their houses that day, which chanced to be the festival of Corpus Domini,*

---

* It fell that year on the 9th of June.

to perform the customary ceremonies. The long procession had scarcely ceased to wind through the narrow streets, when a breathless courier is announced. He is the bearer of all-important tidings—he is admitted to the hastily assembled Senate—he comes from the Pasha of Roumilia, who is in their interest, and now urges them without a moment's delay to send an embassy to the Sultan, suddenly and contrary to all expectation disposed to listen to their overtures. The account given by the Ragusans is as follows:—Mahomet had already mounted to carry his threat into execution, when his horse showed a strange and unwonted disinclination to obey him. Thrice he urged him forward towards the city;—thrice the animal stood as if rooted to the ground. At length, when the fiery Sultan, with his customary impetuosity, would have forced him forward, he reared, plunged, and endeavoured to throw his rider, who declared afterwards that he saw at that moment a figure like the representations of

St. Blaise, the patron saint of the city, for-
bidding him to go forward. . . . . Mahomet
received the deputation kindly, but demanded
the instant cession of their whole territory
except the city itself. "Willingly," was the
reply of the quick-witted Nicolo Serafino di
Bona; "but in that case we must deliver the
city into the hands of the King of Hungary!"
From henceforth they heard no more of surrendering their territory.

After this, Ragusa made great preparations
for defence in case of a future siege, pulled
down the houses in the suburbs, erected new
fortresses and surrounded a greater space
with walls and ditches. They continued,
however, none the less to receive the numerous refugees whether of royal blood or
others, both Slaves and Greeks, who still kept
flocking in on all sides. There were the queens
of Bosnia, the husband of one of whom, named
Stephen, had been flayed alive by the Turks;
the wife of Lazarus, despot of Servia; the old
imperial families, the Lascari, Comneni, Palæo-

logi, and Catecuzenzi, &c., and *literati* of Greece almost innumerable. To all the Senate gave whatever they needed in their destitute condition—asylum, clothes, money, transport. Even yet for a little while Trebigne, Castelnuovo, and a few strong places in the neighbourhood garrisoned by Hungarian troops, held out under the command of the sons of the · Slave prince, Hezegh Stephen,* until Essibeg, sangiac of Triconesi, descended and drove them out. The fugitives betook themselves to Ragusa, where they arrived as private persons. And thus at length, after nine centuries of rule and misrule, fell the bloody and disorderly kingdom of the Dalmatian Slaves, involving in its ruin Ragusa's future hopes whether of territorial aggrandizement or of fresh aggregations to her citizens. Henceforth she must be contented to hold her own, to maintain her independence and

---

* Herzegh or Herzog, German for "Duke," whence his dominions, "the Duchy of Santo Saba," obtained its name of Herzegovina, which it still retains.

Y

trade, to avoid an open breach with the Sultan, and to this end gain his viziers, propitiate his pashas, make friends with his sangiacs, and by whatever efforts maintain herself, what she had been hitherto, the steps of commerce with the Turkish provinces, and her port the main channel with the Levant. Here then was the first cause predisposing Ragusa towards ruin. If it be true that great empires are wont, from the constitution of things, to retrograde so soon as they have ceased to make progress, there is of course no reason why the smallest state, which is complete in itself and independent, should be exempt from the same rule. As it is the nature of all this world's productions to have a period of growth and a moment of perfection, so must they likewise have a period of decay. Not that Ragusa had arrived at this latter as yet; rather it was her zenith and hour of noblest triumph, while she turned her cultivated mind wholly to negotiation and commerce, and as she had before rapidly recovered from the effects of frequent and destructive wars with the Slaves, so now she rose again brighter and higher out of plagues and devastating fires; accommodated herself to the change in her position consequent on the Turkish conquest, turned an accidental collision with Venice to her profit — for while Venice, to revenge an alleged injury at Ferrara,* laid a crushing toll on her ships anchoring in Venetian ports, Ragusa, turning to Egypt and Spain and France and England, only more widely extended her commerce, and having Sicily and Southern Italy and Romagna still open to her near home, left her more powerful rival to learn by experience the bitter fruit of such narrow and short-sighted policy,—

---

* The case was this. Venice had sent her fleet to besiege Ferrara. The papal nuncio, who was in the town, insisted on some Ragusan vessels, which happened to be lying there, taking part in the defence, and the Venetians were repulsed with loss. Venice retaliated on Ragusa, as for a treacherous breach of neutrality, and laid a tax of one hundred ducats of gold on each of her ships which should anchor in a Venetian port. Of course this amounted virtually to exclusion.

her flag sailed across the ocean and appeared in the New World, and her genius, growing with every emergency, triumphed in commerce, in politics, and letters, both at home and abroad.

Venice, humbled by the league, so disastrous for her, of Cambrai, soon removed her unwise edict, and readmitted the Ragusans to their former ample privileges. But notwithstanding this transitory gleam of sunshine, speedily a new and heavier misfortune than any which had gone before fell upon them. The second cause of their decay was at hand. And it is honourable that, while this is the only one of the three which they can be said to have brought upon themselves, it arose from imprudent devotion to the cause of their allies. We have seen that the policy of a small commonwealth like Ragusa, whose main objects were independence and trade, demanded a strict neutrality in the wars of her mightier neighbours, whenever at least her own interests were not primarily con-

cerned; and during the ages of her rise and
first prosperity she adhered to this rule. In
earlier days for the sake of it she had re-
nounced the protection of the eastern Emperors for that of the Norman kings, and later
she had congéd Venice for that of the kings
of Hungary. But now, towards the end of
the fifteenth century, she contracted a very
close alliance with the Spanish monarchs,
with whose country she had her chief commerce. So soon as A.D. 1494 they had, as
already mentioned, undertaken the convoy
of the Moors to Africa from that kingdom,
which so far proved a very lucrative engagement. But later, under Charles V., in his
expeditions against the coast of Africa, and
then under the three Philips, the second, third,
and fourth of that name, in their wars with
France, and England, and Holland, she de-
parted from her original policy, not indeed
avowedly by sending a fleet, but *virtually*
by allowing her naval force to volunteer, and
thus within a few years lost a hundred and

seventy-eight ships, or, including the destruction of their Indian squadron under the command of their captains Martolossi and Masci-
bradi, *three hundred;* so that by the middle
of the seventeenth century her marine was
annihilated and all the flower of the state
cut off.

Immediately upon this came the third and
heaviest blow of all. It was the 6th of
April, A.D. 1667, a fine, calm day; people
had but lately risen, and fires were just
lighted on the kitchen hearths. Some were
already gone to their devotions in the neighbouring churches; others still at home waited
the moment for going out to their customary
avocations, when, without any premonitory
warning whatsoever, a short but strong shock
of earthquake shook the rock to its foundation, and swallowed up or cast down the
whole city except the walls and a few of
the most solid buildings, while five thousand
human beings found themselves in one moment buried in its ruins. Such was the first

and final announcement of the great earthquake! The scene of confusion and horror which followed is best given in the words of the historian Appendini, who gathered it from the contemporary accounts. " Amidst terrific bellowings from the agitated mountain, the ground was felt and even seen to reel and stagger underfoot. The sea was strangely agitated, and the vessels in the haven, either driving one against another, became wrecks, or, if they were far asunder and less affected, dived with their prows under the waves, as if they were going down head-foremost. The water in the harbour, which at first shrank to a quarter of its usual volume, then increased to four or five feet above the high-water mark. A castle on the shore was observed to open and shut its gates three times : the fountains and cisterns became dry: and a dense cloud of dust arose, which obscured the face of the heavens."

The state of those who were not at once covered by the falling ruins, or swallowed

up in the yawning ground, may be imagined.
" Six hundred individuals, who with ghastly
wounds and broken limbs escaped as by a
miracle from beneath the falling edifices,
joined a favoured few, who stood unhurt,
but mute and trembling, in the middle of
the piazza, or square, expecting, so terrible
was the impression left on the nerves by the
first shock, that the end of all things was
at hand! A sort of stupor appeared at the
first moment to fall upon the victims, and
to deprive them of their senses. Then, when
after a few seconds the first feeling of oppres-
sion and terror passed, and, awakening again
to the emotions of compassion, they would
fain have flown to the succour of parents,
wives, children, relations, friends and country,
their strength failed them amidst fresh trem-
blings, or they were themselves in a moment
crushed by the falling rafters, or they saw
their efforts hopeless ; the whole city being
but one mass of stones, the narrow streets
blocked up, and their own habitations no

longer recognisable! From every side issued the agonised shrieks of persons jammed in the ruins, and piteous cries for help at a moment when everyone needed it for himself. Simon Ghetaldi, the rector, several of his family, many senators and patricians, awaiting the opening of the Great Council in the vicinity of the palace; George Crook, Dutch resident for the dominions of the Sublime Porte, with twenty of his suite; two knights of Malta, a German gentleman, and the nuns of St. Mark's, all remained to die miserably under the ruins. The same sad fate overtook a large girls' school, in the neighbourhood of which some days afterwards pitiful groans were still heard, and entreaties for water without any means being found to render the required aid! Nine-tenths of the clergy perished. The archbishop, throwing himself from a window, escaped, not without a severe contusion, in spite of which he contrived to hasten through every practicable part of the city, confessing, absolving, giving his blessing

and inspiring courage to a multitude, who
clung to his vestments as they felt one con-
cussion following another.

"As the lesser shocks died away, a fearful
conflagration broke out, either from the fires
just lighted on the hearths, or from subter-
raneous sources; while a tempestuous wind,
which had suddenly arisen, rolled the dense
volumes of smoke over the still palpitating,
heaving mass of ruins. The wretched survivors
made haste to get on board the ships lying
off Lacroma, expecting the flames to reach
the powder-magazine in the arsenal, which
fortunately, however, was hindered by the
ruins.

"And now, as the flames died away, a
diabolical horde of Morlachs, who had come
to market, uniting with some of the neighbouring peasantry, entered remorselessly into
the town, and there commenced pillaging on
all sides; seizing upon the gold and silver
of the houses, and the richly-mounted re-
liquaries or chalices of the churches, with-

out any one, at the moment, being able to offer effectual resistance. These wretches did not hesitate to murder with their muskets any who came across them in their career of plunder, till the Senate, reduced to twenty-five nobles, who alone survived, aroused themselves, shut the city gates, defeated another and more numerous troop, who were coming down from the hills, and proceeded to excavate such of the sufferers as could be got out. Even until the third day unfortunates continued to be extracted and restored to life...."

In preceding years considerable earthquakes had been twice felt. In A.D. 1520, on the feast of the Ascension, the earth's agitation is said to have been so great that the "Mount Bergato" seemed to bow itself menacingly towards the city. And for twenty months afterwards, houses and churches continued, from time to time, to fall. But only twenty-eight years before, A.D. 1629, the whole city was loosened from its foundations; so that when the last great shock came, the entire town, having probably been weakened previously, fell to the ground with one crash, the most massive buildings, *e.g.* the rectorial palace, barely surviving with the loss of its roof and upper story. For the rest, this earthquake was felt as far as Venice northwards, and to the Morea on the south. It ruined the whole state of Ragusa, and the city of Budua, doing great mischief also at Perasto, Cattaro, Dolcigno, and Antivari, while every Ragusan family mourned some member, and many were reduced to a single scion.*

Such was *the great earthquake*, which made so deep an impression throughout the civilized world at the time, that the memory

---

* Pliny mentions an earthquake as having originally united the sites of ancient Epidaurus and Oricum to the mainland: "Epidaurus et Oricum (propter motum terræ) insulæ esse desierunt." Lib. ii. cap.89. Also, St. Hilarion, in the same country, is related by his prayers to have killed a serpent, and stopped *the invasion of the sea after an earthquake*, in the days of the Emperor Julian, A.D. 365. Cf. Append. Vol. I. Part I. lib. ii. cap. 2 and 6.

of it still lives unobliterated by the yet greater ones at Lisbon (A.D. 1755), and in Calabria (A.D. 1783), which have happened since.

It was mainly owing to the benevolence of Clement IX. that Ragusa rose again from its dust and ashes. The greatest opposition was experienced at Constantinople from the fierce vizier, Carà Mustafà. Four men, whose names* deserve to be written in gold in the annals of the republic, devoting themselves to death, if necessary, for the sake of their country, went to negotiate this for *them* all-weighty affair at the capital of the sultans.   One of these patriots actually completed his self-sacrifice, and died in the fearful dungeon into which, at that time, on the least provocation, or without any, the envoys of Ragusa used to be thrown.   At length they triumphed over all opposition, in spite of the Grand Vizier's hostility, who, a few years later, still breathing threats

* Bona, Gozze, Caboga, Buchia. Two of them were sent to Silistria, and two to Constantinople.

against the republic, to be fulfilled as soon
as he should have taken Vienna, having
failed in that expedition, received the due
reward of his ferocity by the loss of his
head.

Thus Ragusa stood once more. Its constitution was re-established, and in a small
way it again flourished. Some danger still
threatened, and now it was from the opposite
side, namely, from the allied Christian arma-
ment, which, on its road against the Turks,
occupied both by sea and land Castel
Nuovo, and other places bordering on the
territory of the republic. Giorgi, the poet,
was engaged in these negotiations. At
length, at the treaty of Passarovitz,* it
was finally reinstated in its original position,
a free communication guaranteed between
its territories and those of the Sublime
Porte, and, for additional security against

---

* The peace of Passarovitz was negotiated between Venice
and Turkey by the mediation of England and Holland,
A.D. 1718.

Venetian ambition, the contiguity of Veneto-Dalmatia with the state of Ragusa interrupted by bringing the Turkish frontier down to the sea on either side.

By help of the land traffic, which still lasted though falling off, Ragusa even recovered some of its marine, and thus grew rich, especially during the war between England and Spain, when Gibraltar fell into the hands of the former (A.D. 1704). But the losses of the period of the earthquake were irreparable.* Their ships had been previously annihilated, and their maritime commerce was reduced to such an extent, that a few small vessels or "trabaccoli," which kept within the Adriatic, sufficed for it. All the property, which they had with them at home, was burnt, buried, or robbed by the Morlachs, and of that which was

---

* The population of the town, which with the suburbs had been computed at the end of the fifteenth century by Filippo de Quartigianis at forty thousand, was diminished to five or six thousand. It is now not above four thousand at the outside.

abroad, a great deal more was irrecoverably lost to its owners by the circumstance of its lying under false names in the Monti di Pietà — sort of savings' banks — of Italy, where it had been thus invested in order to escape a tax of twenty per cent. laid by the Senate on exported moneys. The depositors being thus suddenly cut off, there was too often no one who knew under what name it stood. Their colonies also were fast disappearing; for instead of going themselves to carry their merchandise, they now chiefly commissioned Turkish agents; and the Turks themselves, no longer as heretofore engaged in constant wars, began to traffic on their own account. Hence, by the end of the eighteenth century, or beginning of the nineteenth, there remained, of all their extended colonies, only two persons in Bosnia, and a house in Barletta, in the kingdom of Naples.

Now, also, the other seeds of internal decay noted above began to come up and bear fruit. The noble and civic families were both dying out. Every year the upper ranks of their population fell off, and there were no means of adding to their numbers as formerly. In A.D. 1800, nearly a hundred families of these privileged classes per century had become extinct for the last six hundred years, while, during at least half that time, the supply by immigration from the surrounding provinces had been cut off, owing to the Turkish and Venetian conquests. About the beginning of this century, or the end of the last, the illustrious families of Palmotta, Gondola, and Giorgi, all came to an end,* and many more, whose names, less known to fame, have not been recorded.

Another calamity worse than extinction itself, was the feud which arose between the Sorbonnesi and the Salamanchesi, and is

* The Palmottas came to an end in the seventeenth century. Ignazio Giorgi was himself the last of his line. Francis Joseph Gondola, Bishop of Paderborn, and the Republic's minister at Vienna, died A.D. 1773; he was the last of that name.

curiously illustrative of the pitch of folly to
which the pride of little distinctions may
lead people. The Salamanchesi were those
honourable *civic* families, who had been aggregated to the patrician order to supply the
gaps caused by the earthquake, and, now
that there were no longer any lords and
princes in Slavonia to increase their numbers, by the natural ravages of time itself.
Amongst these was at one time no less a
name than that of Giorgi, often mentioned
above. The Sorbonnesi, on the other hand,
were the original, old patricians. These
classes, in spite that the state declared them
on an equality with each other, refused to
mix. Whether the Salamanchesi actually
experienced the pride of the Sorbonnesi, or
only suspected it, or however it was, thus
much is certain (though indeed Appendini,
in his panegyrical history, has avoided the
painful subject),* no intercourse could take

* By bringing his narrative to a close with the above-
named peace, A. D. 1718, and leaving the feud unnoticed
elsewhere

place between them. If they met—as meet
they must in the public assemblies—each
side came armed. Should young and inex-
perienced people, unfortunately for themselves, break through the barrier, and unite
in wedlock, they were excluded from the
society of both parties.

Even the *coup de grace*, which came in this
century, must be attributed immediately to
that which has been pointed out as the second
cause predisposing to their ruin, namely, interference in the quarrels of foreign nations. For
when they paid that homage to the great name
of Napoleon I., that they opened their gates
to his troops, notwithstanding a superior force
of Russians and Montenegrins also in the
neighbourhood, and the British navy the mis-
tress of the seas, they were in fact voluntarily taking part in the great strife then
raging in Europe, a perilous task for a small
state such as Ragusa, even in its palmiest
days—how much more so in its weakened
condition during the revolutionary era of the

early half of the nineteenth century! But how might they have done otherwise? This is a question, the solution of which, supposing it to be possible, cannot be attempted here. Such is the simple fact: Ragusa, like its old rival, Venice, voluntarily admitted the French troops, and was favoured to some extent as long as that Government retained possession of it. But thus doing, they rejected a second time their golden rule of non-interference, and, espousing again the side of a vast empire, were drawn finally into the vortex occasioned by its fall.

THE END.

CPSIA information can be obtained
at www.ICGtesting.com
Printed in the USA
FSOW01n0733291116
27939FS